My Journey
By
His Grace

Steve,

Thank you for believing in me. Your support for me and my family means so much. From the heart I pray you are blessed for blessing us. Thanks for being a great leader, friend and brother

With love from the heart

Love
Eric D Faltz

CONTENTS

INTRODUCTION

I t sure is a great day for a great day! The purpose of this book is for me to share my views, feelings and outlook on not only my life but the life of those around me that I love and that love me and simply my encounters in general through my experiences. This book is not intended to talk about anyone, nor to make anyone feel bad about our encounters, it is simply my views personally. Some of you have blessed me and helped change me in ways you wouldn't even know. I do believe that each one of us has something to share to help others to not have to endure the pain of certain mistakes that we make while going through life. If I can help save someone the time and pain of traveling down a road where I found a dead end, I would love to do it. I feel that the next generation can benefit from this book and these thoughts that I have.

I am going to discuss God, failures, success, pain, love, thoughts, fear, anxiety, race, generational cycles, overcoming fear, marriage struggles, friends, family, parenting, grace, mercy, blessings, serving and life in general as I remember it and as I see it. In life we do not know what we do not know. We often judge others based on our views and experiences; however, if someone cannot see your views, they will not be able to see your point, unless explained in a certain manner. There are many of us that walk around thinking we cannot overcome or change our situations and circumstances as they may seem very limited. I am here to tell you that where you are today is not where God intended for you to stay, nor will it be the end of your story unless you allow it to be. Your right now is not you or where you are intended to stay; you may be going through something for you or you may be going through it for someone else. If you want change you will have to fight, grind, push and PRAY your way through the tough times. You will read in this book about how serving others has blessed me and helped me write this book. There were many odds against me completing this book as I never dreamed of writing a book until after years of sharing a daily message to inspire people around me. It is amazing that the same inspiration that I do my best to share with others inspired me to do better and share my experiences with all of you in hopes and prayer that someone will be inspired to overcome an obstacle they are currently facing—if I can do it, you can too. Thank God for His love, His grace and mercy and blessing me to do something that was completely out of my league until I believed. Just like me, you can do it too; the question is will you believe?

If we do not change our thoughts, as thoughts become actions, we will simply recycle our experiences in life. The Bible tells us, "As a man thinks so is he." What are you thinking? I pray this book blesses you as you read the transparent account of how I changed my lens and God changed my life.

1

THE LESSONS BEGIN

As a very young boy I was blessed to be surrounded by a lot of family, I really was. There are a few people in my life who have had a significant impact on me and I am so grateful and blessed to share my life with them. When I was just a young boy, I was able to spend most of my life with my parents, brothers, sisters, grandparents, and great-grandmother. Talk about being blessed with family. I love my grandparents, I really do. I love them for their care, love, knowledge, wisdom and simply their ability to care about everyone's true best interest. I loved it… I have four brothers, three who are older than me, and our mom had my older brothers prior to marrying my dad from her first marriage, I also have two sisters. One of my brothers and one of my sisters I found out about much later in life due to my dad having them outside of his and my mom's marriage (I will get into that later in the book). So that means in our household growing up there were five of us kids and two parents.

Looking back on life growing up, we lived in Reston, Virginia, a neighborhood called Laurel Glade; I will start here as, when I think back, this is where I really remember life's education starting for me. I truly believe there are two different kinds of education in life. There is education in school, which I was never good at. I say that I wasn't ever really good at it because I didn't understand or respect the importance of a school education, nor did I have anyone really pushing me to stay focused on the "why" of school. I don't blame anyone for this as I am my own person and chose my own paths. My mom was busy, as you can imagine; she drove a school bus and took care of the family. My dad was busy working late-night hours as he drove large trucks most of my life. I remember him leaving for work at 1:00–2:00 a.m. every morning and working until the afternoons. This is one of the key values I got from him and that was to work very hard. My dad was also a bit of a partier back in the day. With their schedules it was pretty easy for me to skip school or slack off in life. My mom had to leave earlier in the morning and my dad was long gone by the time we had to get ready for school and my brothers had to wake me up before they went to school. So after they left I was free to do whatever until my mom would come home for her morning break and then I would play sleep/sick and then it was too late for me to go to school by the time her break was over. I didn't skip a lot, but, as you can see, there was a lot of room for me to goof off. This is probably the biggest area outside of my relationship with God that I wish I had focused on and taken more seriously in my life.

As a young boy I always wanted to own my own company and become the CEO of it. What I didn't do was share that dream enough for someone who knew better to educate me in whatever some of the most successful CEOs were educated in. That is where I had big dreams but couldn't connect the "how to" to them. Again, this was just me as a young boy having dreams. Laurel Glade taught me how to hustle. When I mention hustle, I am not talking about drugs, I am simply talking about the hustle of life and getting educated in how the streets work and, of course, how they don't work.

In our neighborhood we had a candy lady (who lived in the apartments) and a candy man who would drive around one of those box step vans and sell a lot of food items. We also had an ice cream man, who came around twice a day, and a seafood truck that came around once a week if I remember correctly. This was all in the apartment complex where we lived in a three-bedroom apartment. Yes, that is correct; seven people living in this apartment, two parents and five children. Oldest to youngest, we were Mike, Derrick, Shawn, Eric (me), and Lydia. Needlessly to say, it was very crowded and there was a lot of drama—A LOT! So, with all that going on and my parents doing their best to take care of us we were strapped for money and we made decisions more on a "do you need it" than a "do you want it" mindset. So, as you can tell, I needed to hustle at an early age to ensure I had some money for all these vendors that were around us. I loved me some sweets and pickles, chips, soda, all of it... Man, those were the days... The candy man was my favorite, he was the coolest. I could get on his truck with a dollar or two and come back with a bunch of junk food. He really looked out for me and my hustle as a young boy. He sold candy, gum, pig feet (which I do not eat—yuck), pickles, chips, and sodas, all that on one truck, and he came around daily right around the time the sun was setting. I remember he used to drive around and blow his horn to let everyone know he was there. I can still hear it now... I remember I used to run to that truck so fast and get in line, a lot of time being the first one in line waiting on him.

So back to the hustle part, I would do just about anything (legal) for a quarter or a dollar, it didn't matter; I learned at a very young age how to make money. What I didn't do was learn how to save it. Making money without learning to save it will keep you busy with the exchange of having to make more just to give it out. I would run messages for people, take out their trash, clean up, just about anything. I remember working on Paul's ice cream truck to make a few bucks to buy ice cream and spend my money right back on his truck. It was as if I was working for ice cream. Paul had a serious hustle going on. I remember he always had a bundle of cash. He would pull his stack of cash out of his pocket; it was so big that he could barely get it out. I am very surprised he didn't get robbed often due to having so much cash in that area back in the '80s in the area we lived in. The candy lady, she had bunches of candy and pickles, hot sausages, etc. She lived right in the neighborhood so we could just go to her apartment and buy things. Needless to say I had plenty of reasons to hustle to make some money and a bunch of reasons to spend all the money I made. I couldn't make the money fast enough, but again I learned how to make and spend and hustle to get more.

Laurel Glade had a bunch of things that would carry on, drugs, guns, gambling, drama, love, partying, fighting, etc. One of my brothers, Mike, he was much older than me, he was the oldest of us all. Mike was really the first person I paid close attention to as one of my brothers that went out into the world and started to make a way for himself. He would hang out with his friends as they were tougher than most around the neighborhood. Mike is a good person and has really been impactful in my life as my big brother. Like many others in the neighborhood, he didn't have much direction or guidance. He had to figure out his way in life and some of it, being the oldest and first one out of the house, wasn't always the best decisions (I am sure). I remember being a young boy and watching my parents not really coach Mike as much as they could, they were more corrective than anything. This is just how it was back in the day. Parents didn't seem to give you direction as much as they corrected you to tell you what not to do. I remember my brothers getting whippings back in the day enough to know that wasn't for me at all. Back then, it was allowed, and parents didn't get in trouble for it. I got two major whippings that I remember throughout my life and boy did they hurt.

Mike was the first person I ever witnessed falling in love. I was way too young to understand love, what it meant, or how it makes us feel. I watched Mike continue to learn the streets and the ins and outs. He had a very close friend and he was wild; he wasn't afraid of anything that I ever witnessed. This guy could fight and wasn't afraid to do so. I remember being at home one night and they got into a fight at the local carnival that would come around every now and then and somebody hit Mike's friend in the head with a bottle and hurt him pretty bad. I remember my mom got the call to go help him. She was always cool this way. She was there for everyone all the time as much as she possibly could have been. That is one thing that has always been very special about our mother. That event at the carnival with them was one of the few incidents that was scary for me as a young boy, but life had to go on. It is very strange how we get used to our surroundings no matter how crazy they may seem to the people who don't have to deal with them.

One night, while I was sleeping (I was told the story the next day), our mother heard someone yelling Mike's name outside and thought it was to my brother and it wasn't, but as she looked out the window someone shot a gun and by mistake the bullet came through my parents' bedroom window while my mom was looking out of it, the bullet just missed her. She knows who it was, but it was a young man we all knew of, so she didn't say anything. It was a true accident to everyone's knowledge. He was never arrested or anything. There was another one of our neighbors that lived on the bottom floor a couple of buildings over; someone climbed in his bedroom window and cut him around his neck area in an attempt to kill him. He lived, but again scary stuff as a kid. In Reston we had many laughs and great times as well. We used to play tag and climb trees, ride bicycles, make friends, snow sled, run, and laugh and play on playgrounds and take the bus to the mall.

The mall visit was one of my first times making a big mistake in life and boy did I pay for it. My friends and I started to think it was a good idea to steal items we didn't have money for. We decided to take the bus from Reston to Tyson's mall and steal some things out of stores. Was that ever a mistake! We got to the mall and I remember stealing right out of the stores, cassette tapes and some other items. We made it all the way back home and like most people we started to brag about our successful stealing mission and my brother Derrick decided to tell our parents on us. Did this ever hurt! My dad came home and put a very serious whipping on me and threw the items I stole in the trash. This was the first serious whipping I received in my life. It hurt and I hoped that I would never receive another one of those in life. I still remember that day. I would like to say it made me never steal again, but that isn't the truth. It made me learn how to keep my mouth shut and not tell anyone whenever I did wrong.

2

GRANDMA FOLKS' HOUSE

A round this time in life I believe I was in the fourth grade give or take. I didn't spend much time with my dad as a kid, he will tell you to this day he was all about women, money, partying and, truth be told, himself. We would take weekend trips to my dad's parents' house. Grandma Henrietta Folks (Grandma Folks), Elisha Folks Sr. (POP). This is where I spent most of my time just spending some time with my dad, although we did not spend direct time together there. He would do the adult things, while I spent time running around with my cousins having a good time. We had so much fun and every now and then some drama would happen there. I did a lot there and learned a lot there about relationships and the real reason to treat everyone equal and fair. My dad has two sisters and for a lot of my life they lived with my grandma (their mother) on and off and when they would move out or away, their kids (my cousins) would stay there a lot.

My grandma's house was the place to be on a weekend. That is where I got my true love for cars and watched people come together in fun and help each other. My dad would meet his uncles there and work on cars and things of that nature. They would share stories and drink beer, smoke and whatever else they did, they were so awesome to watch. Talk about fun and laughing and joking. They had a blast and you could tell just being there. I could tell my grandma loved it as well, her family coming around to have a great time and help around her house while they were there. I remember Uncle Raymond working around her house with light fixtures and ceiling fans. I do not remember much about him as I was young when he passed away; however, he used to drive a big brown bronco and smoke a pipe that smelled awesome. I can still remember the smell to this day. He had the loudest laugh and voice and didn't mind telling you exactly what was on his mind if he thought you were out of yours. We didn't talk often as he was always talking with the grownups; however, he would say hello coming and going. If my dad and his uncles didn't have the answer to a problem someone else did; I saw pain, love, fighting, and celebrating happen there.

Grandma's house was in Fairfax Station, VA. They had a nice house with a big yard and all. We would have family reunions, parties, cookouts, etc. One of the greatest things I remember was riding in the car to their house. I loved to ride in cars as a young kid. We would stop at a convenience store and get a soda and some candy and those were the days. That may not seem like much to some kids today, but it was everything when I was young. Riding in the cars with the windows down and the radio playing was amazing in those times of my life, I still love it today.

One time when I was a young boy, my grandfather (Pop) whom I didn't have a good relationship with (how does a boy not have a good relationship with his grandad?) and my dad got into a huge fight. My dad was quiet but had a serious temper if it was pushed beyond the limit as a lot of us do. It was about something very stupid, like my uncle moved something in Pop's shed and he went off bad on my uncle verbally. He was a veteran from WWII who drank quite a bit. My dad snapped and I remember my family being there and my dad tried his best, being held back (thank God), to get to Pop's gun supply. I truly believe until this day my dad would have shot his very own dad. There obviously had to be more to it than that night and some items being moved in a shed, but that is the tricky thing about life, we carry hurt, pain and burdens with us and sometimes it builds up like pressure in a pipe until it explodes just like a pipe does and we release that pressure on another human being, sometimes on the ones we love. My dad never mentioned this day again and I never asked about it as I knew better after seeing the explosion of that pain that was being carried. I am not sure about Pop's life prior to this time and me witnessing this issue other than his mother died at a young age, he dropped out of school very young and that his dad wasn't a nice man to my knowledge, which could explain a lot. I didn't learn this until years after Pop passed away.

Think about this from a generational standpoint, my great-grandad (whom I didn't know) wasn't a nice man to his kids, Pop had many struggles and my dad had some serious struggles as well. Is it a surprise that you will read that I struggled as well? This is a deep view into our family's history, imagine what the future would hold if change didn't happen. I wasn't Pop's favorite or even liked at this point is how I felt as a little kid. He had two grandsons, me and my older cousin Thomas who was about a year older than me. This part of my life was painful for me and I still don't understand it, but I have forgiven and moved on.

Thomas was painfully and obviously Pop's favorite. Sometimes I wasn't really acknowledged by Pop. I am not sure exactly why and never really dove into it. I always just assumed because my dad was in my life, he didn't think I needed the attention. You see Thomas's parents were divorced. I am not saying anything is wrong with that, just explaining or justifying why my grandad didn't care for me for a lot of my years. Sometimes we need to justify why we think someone is a certain way, but the truth is we end up making excuses for behavior that is not right sometimes. Pop would always be there for Thomas and buy him things—mopeds, dirt bikes—and give him money, etc.

Thomas's dad was in his and his sister's life, he was a good man and every now and then he would allow me to go with them on events and day trips to hang out. He always treated me with much respect and made me feel very much like family to him. Thomas was the coolest cousin, he really was. I looked up to him and he always was ahead of me in life. Music, movies, girls, motorized vehicles, working on vehicles. This guy could take apart anything and I needed to learn a few things from him. I remember Thomas hooking up a car stereo and speakers with a car battery on a wagon that you pull with your hand when we were young, he had skills at a young age. Thomas appeared to be fearless as I was the little cousin looking up to him. He and I spent quite an amount of time growing up from little kids all the way to late teenage years. He taught me a bunch from playing in the sand box with Tonka trucks to how to drive when I was 13, how to install a stereo in a car, how to ride a moped/motorcycle and install lights on cars, which is a passion for me now as an adult. I remember one time our grandma told us not to leave the yard and we did anyway, and Thomas and I were on his moped and I wrecked it into a creek. We laughed about this for years, it was dangerous as we rode motorized machines with no helmets, when I got thrown off the moped into the creek anything could have happened. We didn't worry about the dangers back then. There is something about when we are disobedient to our elders life has a way of teaching us. There was a bunch that he taught me.

Pop used to work at a junk yard called Penny's and we would go to work with him sometimes when I was there on the weekends. We would go help a little bit and they would pay us a few dollars for spending the day down there. That is where I drove my first car, that is also the first car I wrecked and drove the entire side down another vehicle at the junk yard. They weren't happy about it, but I learned what not to do while driving. Pop used to work seven days a week for Penny's, he would rarely take a day off or time to himself, he was working all the time. Just like the hustle I learned from my dad to grind, Pop had that same hustle and grind. A couple of times a year he would clean up his nice car and head somewhere in the southern states, North Carolina, I think, I never really knew. Grandma never went with him or even asked when he would return. He just left and came back whenever. Every evening, when Pop came home from work, he would stop at the little store called High's and play lotto and pick up candy for most of the grandkids that were at their house. He would always stop at the end of the driveway and the girls (cousins) would run to the end of the driveway and jump on the back of his ranchero to drive up the driveway. From what I could tell this was Pop's way of showing them love. I remember going to Pop to ask him for something and he would deny it to me and then my cousin Thomas would go directly behind me and get what I just asked for. I never really understood that part, as a child it hurt my feelings big time. My mom would notice it but never said anything directly to him. I remember one time my grandma witnessed it directly, not that she didn't the other times, but for some reason she decided to confront him about telling me he didn't have any money and Thomas went right to him and he gave it to him. When she asked about what he did, he denied it. It was a strange moment, but it kind of aired the issue in my eyes.

My grandma had some similar issues with her kids and grandchildren. It was almost as if everyone couldn't be treated equally, she always had to have a favorite as well. This is something that I am still puzzled about. It was clear she had a favorite child. It was very obvious as she would do anything for her, I do mean anything. I remember being a little boy and Grandma would need something, whether it was help around the house or money to pay a bill; my dad would be there for her as much as he could even though we had major financial struggles in our own home. My mom never said anything as she knew he supported his mom's family/house as well. My dad would never speak with her about the favoritism that took place, but, truth be told, I don't think it would have made a difference. There came a time in my life when I couldn't take it anymore and she got after me for doing something and only said something to me and not my other cousins that she favored so much at the time and I actually said something to her about how she treated me and my sister different. She disciplined me for it; it was worth it because it was on my mind and I had had enough of it. Nothing changed right away from this. I felt a bit better for finally letting it out.

The favoritism was bad and obvious during Christmas time as my sister and I would get no presents from her like the others would. It was a rough feeling as a kid. Little did I know that later in life she and I would have an awesome relationship. She was the initial person, to introduce me to our Lord and Savior Jesus Christ. She was so committed to going to church every Sunday and faithful doing it. I am not sure what happened with her and Pop's marriage; however, they didn't share the same room or the same bed. It was almost as if they didn't like each other but stayed together just because. There was no love in the air at their house as in feelings. They barely had conversation my whole life that I can remember. They would ask each other a question and give an answer and that was it. I heard rumors from people that they used to fight pretty bad before I can remember. Pop would come home and go in his room and stay there. I am talking every day and every night. He never came out into the living room and just sat down or in the kitchen or dining room. This included when my dad and his uncles (Pop's brothers-in-law) would come around and work around the house, he didn't hang out with them much or anything that I remember. I was always worried about this kind of relationship not communicating with your spouse or your family. It seemed so lonely. I couldn't see how two people could be married, love their family and each other (in their own way) but rarely speak any words to each other. I never wanted a relationship like this ever.

Grandma was one of the hardest workers I ever seen in my entire life. I never saw her take a vacation or days off without being really sick and I can't even remember a time that happened. She was a school bus driver for 30 years give or take. She would get up in the morning and get her bus going and come back and wake up my cousins for school and go back out. During her break I remember she would do laundry and watch *The Young and the Restless* (a TV soap opera series). She would cut the grass, cook, clean, work, kill snakes, shoot squirrels with her BB gun because they would eat her trash cans, take out the trash, and take care of the entire family. She was an amazing woman; I didn't appreciate how much she did until later in my life. It was obvious grandmas were so special back then in the African American communities. They were really the glue that held families together. They were like counselors, teachers, and shared so much love from their history of knowledge and wisdom. That all started to change as generations changed over time that I have seen. Grandmothers just didn't and do not seem the same as they were back when I was growing up. It is almost as if the times changed and most are too busy now days holding their homes and families together, working, resting, and living.

Grandma and I started to develop a relationship really after that episode of me speaking my mind. My sister Lydia and I always showed her much more respect than some of the other grandchildren that she seemed to like more than us; however, I knew doing the right thing would pay off eventually. I tried to live most of my life "doing the right thing". I learned early in my life to respect people no matter what. My mom was the one who taught me this. It wasn't through words it was through actions; my mom was always the one to turn away from things that didn't produce anything positive. So later in life we worked on our relationship. It wasn't something we talked about; it was just something we did. I am not sure what changed her mind or helped her start to treat me better, but it was something. We never talked about it, we just moved forward with life. I did help Grandma with some things as I saw her always working so hard and a lot of people around her just kind of letting her. I ended up going to high school near to her house because I didn't like the schools where my parents lived. She gave me my first car. It was a used car that she had bought many years prior brand new, but it meant so much to me that she would give me a car. She had many grandchildren she could have given it to; however, she chose me. I was so honored and treated this car like gold. It was a 1987 Nissan Stanza. My first true car love. It wasn't the car as much as it was the love behind it. You see I found out over the years that my dad's family didn't say the words, "I love you," it was almost as if it was really hard to say, they would care for you or give you things to say how much they loved you. This was tough to understand as a kid; however, like most things in life, kids adapt to it and move forward through life even if unanswered questions stay in their minds.

We got closer and closer over the years. I could talk with her about anything, which was cool—girls, cars, life. You could tell she didn't really want to talk about certain things some of the time, but she would listen and really agree with me most of the time. She was really the person who would agree with what I wanted to hear and not tell me what I really should have heard about right and wrong. We got close throughout my high school years, I loved her so much and she loved me so much I could tell. I would tell her, "I love you," and she would say, "Um huh." I always knew deep down inside she did love me; she just couldn't find the words or say them.

My dad and I weren't close until later in my years as a teenager. I never heard the words, "I love you," from my dad until I was around 15 years old that I remember. It was very tough for him to show love as he was never really shown what love really is. We became close once I started driving as he was really into auto mechanics all my life and we finally had something we could do together or at least discuss. Once I got into the stereos and mechanics of the car thing he really took interest. We wouldn't work on the cars together, but I would mess things up and he would have to help me fix them. I would also hang around and watch him work on cars. This was the beginning of me loving cars and starting to understand how things worked with the mechanics of them. I always knew my dad had my back, but I didn't realize we would be best friends one day. He faced some serious generational cycles that needed to be broken by someone and I have been determined they must be broken with me, right here and right now. Passing on the very pain that hurt me so bad has to stop at all cost. Most of these issues are choices. Once we acknowledge the pain it is easier to recognize and to stop. I have seen too many people in my lifetime that do not understand the importance of change. After all, if nothing changes, nothing changes.

3

Mom's Love, Commitment, Family Struggle

My mother's side of the family was the complete opposite. My mother loves the world and the people in it. She is the sweetest, nicest, kindest person I've known in my life. She is the type that puts others first and thinks about herself last. I know my mother loves all her children, and when I was growing up, she would not only say it, but it is something I felt more than anything. As a young man I watched my mother stay committed to my dad no matter what he was or wasn't doing. I used to wonder why she stayed married to him and I never asked; it was just something I witnessed and kept to myself. My dad was really grouchy to a lot of people and wouldn't think about the things he said before he said them to people including my mother. When I was a young boy, I remember going through my dad's wallet and finding a note from our neighbor, who was my mom's best friend. It appeared to be a love note and my mom had obviously seen the note, and this caused a major problem at the time. My parents did work through this and many other issues that they came across while being married, which included my dad having an affair when I was a very young baby and having children with another woman while married. I would later understand how something like this can easily happen when you are not happy in your current household no matter how good your wife and family life appear to be to others. These are my brother and sister that I have grown to know and love as an adult; however, as a kid there was so much confusion in all our lives. I remember my mother opening a letter in the mail and it was addressed to my dad and it was possibly from Child Support. It appeared there was a third child who was around the age of one of my younger sister Lydia. You see my mom appeared to get over my dad's affair; however, this would mean somewhere around six plus years later my dad was still having an affair. This time in my life was confusing, but I learned a very valuable lesson from this experience (not at this time in my life), much later this would be a lesson I could learn from. My mom loved my dad so much despite the odds that were against her. She was completely as committed as anyone I have ever seen committed in my lifetime. I am blessed to have seen this firsthand and to know my mom had what it took to see her marriage through thick and thin and for better or worse.

I could tell that my dad's family didn't care too much for my mom back then. I couldn't put my finger on why throughout my childhood. It was one of those things no one had to say, you just felt it. Later in life all this changed, and they loved her as if she was one of their own. This time in my mom's life I could tell it was crushing her. I was young, nothing I could say; nothing I could do. I really didn't understand what it all meant. Being so young I only thought about myself and what having brothers and sisters would do or take away from the little bit I thought I had at the time. My dad did not view my brothers and sister in a loving way or anyway that I could tell or see from my view. I had no idea the impact this would have on our future as brothers and sisters. He didn't really acknowledge them in my opinion unless it was when I wasn't around. I didn't get the pleasure of growing up with them at all. I don't think I even really met them until I was either an adult or very close to adulthood. I thought as a young boy, not being shown any better or knowing any different, that this was okay. Little did I know how important they would become to me later in life and how complicated it would be to try to start to have a relationship with them. We really love each other I can tell; however, it is difficult to have a relationship and commit to meeting up in person. I think it is just because we grew up without each other and we are all quiet in our own ways; kind of like our dad we have all gone our separate ways on our very own missions. It is very hard to put into words even as I write this book. I do not like it and we have spent some time together. It is all love while we are together; however, we don't make any efforts to keep it going together.

4

THE DIFFERENCE

It is amazing how different my mom's and my dad's side of the family were growing up. My mom's mom is Grandma Shirley Proctor and her dad, my grandad, is named Earnest Proctor (Papa). Spending time with my mom's parents (my grandparents) was so very different and peaceful. Grandma Shirley is deep and always has been, she would tell you how much she loved you in a heartbeat, but she didn't take no mess and she didn't have no problem letting any of us know that. Papa was so nice and humble, he was one of the most laid-back men I have ever known in my entire life, he was humble, he was so respectful and respected; I learned so much, not from what he said but by his actions. My sister and I would go over to Capital Heights, Maryland to their home and spend some time during our school break in the summer sometimes. They lived with their sister and brother. Our aunt and uncle. The wild thing about this is that Grandma Shirley and her sister married two brothers. Is that wild or what? There were always some cousins over their house just like my Grandma Folks' house. Grandma Shirley was the type of grandma who would plan out the days and have us doing little projects like puzzles, word games, and crafty things, which was great and different in an awesome way. The difference was that she would keep a close eye on us and not just let us roam wild. It was cool but different. I don't remember any of the fussing and fighting that happened at Grandma Folks' house happening at Grandma Shirley's house. I am sure it happened, I just don't remember it being so; we spent much less time there than at Grandma Folks'. Where they lived there always was something going on out in the streets—race cars, wild stories, cool neighbors—it was just busy around there. At their home there was a lot of love and no favorites; this meant if you were wrong, you were wrong no matter who you were and no one had a problem telling you that you were in the wrong and then we would reset and go back to playing just like we should have. That explains the difference of how one grandparent's house could be so filled with love and the other had such a struggle with love.

My mom's dad "Papa" was so laid back and didn't say much. I don't think my entire life I heard him raise his voice or get upset at anyone or anything. He always shook my hand and asked how I was doing. It was such an awesome feeling to know he cared for me transparently and he never said it or had to say it again, it was something I could just feel. We weren't close, but again I learned so much from him, not from anything he said but what he did with his actions. I learned later in life that he was a praying man and maybe that is why he was so calm and humble.

Grandma Shirley, much like Grandma Henrietta later in life, I could talk about anything with. She has been such a supporter to me and even today we sit and talk about God and my walk with Him and her walk with Him as well. It feels so great being able to share stories with her, and we can talk for hours; she shares so much wisdom and love with me. This is what we need more of these days, others to speak about their journey while we listen. I honestly believe this will help a lot of us advance through life and get closer to God because many people at the end of their lives decide to get closer to God. My question is and was if most of us are going to feel the need at some point, later for some, why not do it now? I am so thankful to both of my grandmothers and my mother for helping me connect with God to have a relationship. I truly know and believe that this has been the difference for me in my life keeping me grounded. From my grandmothers going to church on Sundays to my mother saying her prayers every night that I can remember as a child, it has connected me and changed the path of my life and helped me become the man I am today.

5

THE CONNECTIONS WE HAVE

It's strange throughout my life how I have watched how different people connect at different times in their life depending on the stages of life we are going through. This would happen between my brothers, sisters and me. There was a time in my life when my brother Mike and I were close and then a later time Derrick and I would be close and then Shawn and me. Our sister Lydia and I were always close growing up because we were close in age. Our close times come and go and it's strange how we don't always stay in communication. Sometimes we can go months without talking and I can't really understand it but haven't taken the necessary steps to fix it either. That is strange. There was one time when we were hanging out tight in my adult years and I know she loves me, and I know she knows I love her; it is just something that we have never connected for a long time. Our relationship stays true, but communication comes and goes with closeness over time. We are on two different missions in life as she is busy with her life and I am busy with mine. Lydia has a son (my nephew), Cardian, who she loves and adores, she is doing her best to be a great mom to him and I love her for that.

My brother Shawn (third oldest brother) has always been fearless, even as a young boy I watched him take on anything that got in his way whether it was someone physically threatening him or mentally challenging him, he was amazing to watch growing up and didn't nobody want problems with him. We were really close on and off throughout my childhood and we still are even now as adults. There is one thing; he had my back growing up and I am very grateful. If someone were to mess with me, they had to mess with him and that was a fact. Shawn was amazing in basketball, he's a natural that is for sure and he loved the game and could outplay many. I remember being young wishing I had the skill he did on the court. He would play from sunup to sundown and that was daily for many years. Shawn could have easily gone pro if he stayed in the game, sometimes in life we decide to go different routes and no matter how much skill we have or don't have we simply change directions. Shawn has four kids, three boys and one daughter.

My brother Derrick (second oldest brother) was so smart and into school being young, he was the type that stayed studying and passing his classes. Derrick and I have alike personalities when it comes to work and dedication and determination for succeeding in multiple areas of our lives. We have remained the closest out of all my brothers as adults. He is the type I can pick up the phone and call at any moment and he will be there for me for whatever I need as all my brothers would be. Derrick currently works three jobs and is one of the hardest working people I have known in my entire lifetime.

Mike is the oldest out of us all and has grown so much. I am extremely proud of him and what he has accomplished in life. He is married to Robin, who was his longtime girlfriend and has been there for him through thick and thin throughout a lot in this lifetime. They have a daughter, Kylie (Mike's stepdaughter), and a son, Damian. Mike and I have been close on and off for a lot of years but when we weren't the closest we still had mad love for each other. Mike has been there for me in more ways than a little brother could ever ask. This includes Robin as well; she has been supportive and helped me throughout the years.

6

THE LACK OF ALIGNMENT

As I grew up, I would wonder what life would be like and how it would be different if I had a different life. I think a lot of people do that and it isn't uncommon. It isn't that I didn't appreciate what I had, but there seemed to be so much more to life. I have what I think of as a gift to put myself in other people's shoes and it helps me care for others. When they are in pain, I can feel their pain; when they experience joy, I can feel their joy. I would sit and daydream about what life could be like going to the beach or not having to grind it out working to have some cash. My parents did the very best they could, and I am so grateful for them and all they did. So I learned to focus on what I have/had vs. what I didn't. This helped me in many ways not to focus on the bad but focus on the good, and, truth be told, as much as I didn't think I had growing up I always had just enough to make it through, as God has been there every step of the way.

I struggled through school so much, half of it was application; I didn't apply myself as I should have to take the time to understand half of the subjects that we studied in school. I honestly believe I had A.D.D growing up. I would much rather have been outside climbing a tree than in a classroom, learning. I think there were a lot of boys back then who would have preferred to be outside running around instead of in the classroom. Mine was different, though, even when I did apply myself, I couldn't retain a lot of the information that was being presented. Unless the subject was something I was into I simply couldn't program my brain to get interested. I barely passed classes in school most of my life. My parents weren't huge on making sure we got great grades or pushing me for good grades. It was almost as if we had a silent agreement to do my best and make sure I graduated school. At times it was embarrassing to not understand subjects and retain the materials we worked on. I knew this would be a serious problem at some point in school and if I were going to graduate, which is something I was going to do, I would run into a roadblock at some point. I felt as though I had a learning disability when it came to schoolwork, but I would never admit this or bring it up to anyone, being afraid of being made fun of. I knew in order to get through school I was going to have some serious work to do; if I couldn't retain the work and then I was lazy on homework and things of that nature because I didn't understand it most of the time, I would have some serious mountains to climb in the future. All of the classes that were hands-on like shop, auto mechanics, basic math, and science I could get through, but English, history, and social studies, I had absolutely no interest in and I wasn't sure how I was going to get through them, but some way I had to.

My friends would pass their classes with ease; I just couldn't. I believe I struggled so much because I never got the basics of school and I didn't take the extra time that I should have to try harder. I learned later in life that there is no easy road to success; that when climbing the ladder to success any rung that is skipped on the way up will have to be revisited on the way back down even if it is to revisit that rung and continue climbing up. Did I find out later in life how true this is.

There is something else in life that I learned later, that although education and school is so important to our lives, it wouldn't keep me from being successful as success is measured in multiple ways and each of us has to find out what success really means to us. I remember seeing the movie *Boyz n the Hood* as a young kid. This was way before I was supposed to know anything about this type of living and life, not to mention the violence and language; however, one of the many lessons I learned from this movie was that no matter what my background may or may not have been, if I chose to do the right thing and work hard at life I could become successful depending on what I chose to do with my life. It was weird how I could watch movies and retain every scene and even quote them word for word by watching and hearing, but I couldn't do this by listening or by reading for school. It was as if I had to see it in action and then I could remember it step by step. I watched that movie time and time again throughout the years, understanding that being a single father was not an easy life; however, it really set the stage for me to understand the difference between some children and what it meant to have a father present and what it meant to some to not have a father present in their life. It also demonstrated how a family can fuss and fight (just as mine did) yet love and protect and even kill for each other. I loved this movie so much I said, "When I grow up and have a child of my own, I want to name my son Trey." I did just that very thing when my son was born.

I knew that if I was going to be successful in business I would need to find something to focus on and become good at it to compensate for my lack of education. This is where cars came into my life and I started to understand how they operate, how and why. I remember being a young kid and watching the people around me who had nice cars and motorcycles and I thought the world of them, not to say that I wanted theirs, but I wanted to know how could I get my own just like them. That is where I learned to get inspired before getting jealous. There was nothing like a nice car with a good sounding exhaust, nice stereo and a beautiful day outside. I watched older people time and time again and this was going to be my path to success. As I learned about cars, I would start to work on them just a little bit, again watching my dad with his background and his uncles all I had to do was listen and learn. As I learned how to do the basics—oil changes, brakes, stereos, and adding lights—I loved to understand how all of these things worked and didn't work. I found out later I liked troubleshooting. I almost think now, looking back, if I took school seriously, I probably could have been an engineer of some kind. Cleaning them was a huge passion for me as well. Nothing like a nice clean car—wow! It made me feel a certain way. This is where my cousin Thomas and I would take it to the next level many years later. He had a better understanding of how they worked, I watched him for years working on things.

7

THE START

We used to hang with our Aunt Kathy (one of my dad's sisters, everyone called her Kacky). She was really the coolest aunt back them. We would hang out, go to the movies, go bowling, etc. she would always keep her cars clean and stay on top of them when it came to windows being tinted and stereo systems that were loud and sounded good. It was awesome to roll with her. You couldn't tell me and Thomas anything when we were with her. This was something else that was special to being around Grandma Folks' house as Kacky lived with her a lot of my life on and off and there was something always going on around her. She was so fun to kick it with. We would play music, dance, clean cars, play ball, and ride out together. Kacky seemed to always date certain guys that were into cars, racing, stereos, trucks, you name it from an automotive reference, and they were into it. Sometimes we would go to Budd's Creek raceway, which is now known as MIR (Maryland International

Raceway). These are things we would do as a family, my mom/dad, brothers, sister, aunts, uncles, cousins... We would have such a blast going to these events. They would be all-day events. Cleaning up the cars, driving over there, stopping to get buckets of chicken at Kentucky Fried Chicken to eat. They seem like such simple events; however, these were some of the highlights of my childhood. She would also take us roller skating a lot of the time, she was just the coolest of the cool. As you can tell, Kacky was quite the exciting person to be around as a teenager for me. She would call me her son, and it was an amazing feeling to be wanted by someone I looked up to as fun.

Someone else who really has been an important part of my life and influence is my uncle Tony (Big Dipper—that is his street name). Tony is my mom's brother. He looked out for me throughout the years and just like Kacky he taught me a bunch growing up. Tony was and is the uncle I could talk about anything with. I mean anything... He introduced me to girls and just by being around him I started to get an understanding of what life with girls could be like. We had a great time while I was growing up. I would see Tony on and off as he was busy with life, but when I did see him, it was all love. He was fun to be with and cool. He knew about trucks and race cars. A weekend hanging with him was so much fun. We would go to the mall and walk around have a great time flirting with girls and being silly. I remember the very first time I was with a girl he was the first person I called. I am very grateful to have him in my life. We still have that same relationship today and it has only grown stronger and our love has grown. We still talk about anything and everything in life that we feel like discussing with no filters. Our discussions have changed from all fun and girls to marriage, relationships, morals, and God and His word and love.

I was around 13 years old when my first nephew was born. Shawn Nicholson Jr. I was in middle school and I remember hanging with him when he would come over for the weekends as he was a baby and my mom would pick him up. It was so nice to hang with him and even wake up some late nights to feed him or hang with him until he fell back asleep. I thought of how important my uncles were to me and I could help make a difference in his life and be that cool uncle like my uncle Tony was for me. I took a lot of pride in being there for him throughout the years. I had a special relationship with each of my nephews back then. It was important to me to be someone they could look up to even at a young age. Sometimes in life I learned that I could discuss things with my uncles that I could never discuss with my parents at the time.

My first job was at the roller-skating rink in Manassas. It was a place where we would hang on the weekends so I thought having a job there on the weekends would be a great idea. This was where I learned the responsibility of having a job. This was before I was old enough to drive. It was a great place to start. I learned about customer service and really worked at a place I enjoyed. Everyone there already knew who I was, it was a good fit. I remember moving to Manassas, back to West Gate (neighborhood), and going to Stonewall High School for a little while. This was before I had my license or a car and there was a war going on inside of this school between different races... I didn't go to this school long before I asked my parents if I could go live at Grandma Folks' house during the week and go out there on the weekends in order to make sure I was as good as possible in school. This was not a school I wanted to go to, and these battles were not something I wanted to be a part of. They agreed and I left Stonewall. We had lived in Manassas before when I was younger, so I knew a lot of people there, but I just couldn't get involved in anything like that. For the most part of my life I stayed away from bad situations knowing they weren't for me; however, I still got myself into a few jams growing up.

So, I moved back to my grandparents' and went to school there. This was a time when no one else lived there except for Pop and Grandma. I ended up linking back up with Tony Harris who became my best friend while I was living in his neighborhood. The wild thing is that Tony's family was like family to me. His parents knew my grandma Folks, they had spent many years knowing each other. Prior to us moving back to Manassas we lived in the same row of townhouses as Tony's family. I learned so much from the Harrises growing up. They had a tight family and were hugely into sports. His parents always treated me like family. When I didn't have the resources to go out for a weekend, they would help me out and make sure I was good. This family looked out for each other in great ways that helped me understand what a family should do and how selfless people can be. They looked out for others who struggled to look out for themselves. I have a ton of respect for them and always will.

Mr. Harris (Tony's dad) would go to the library for a class every week, I believe it was Tuesdays, and he would allow us to go with him most of the time. Mr. Harris was a humble and quiet man back then that always appeared to handle his business and he still is today. It was nice to get out of the house even to hang at a library. You would think I was there studying and catching up on work, which most people do. Nope, I was there watching TV and goofing around. Tony, his younger brother and I would have a blast hanging out there. We spent a couple of years living in this neighborhood near the Harrises and I was just like family to them. Even to this day I still feel like they are family to me. I don't see them often these days but being that tight isn't something you do simply because we are there in a physical form. I had also gone to elementary school with them when I was younger, so again we knew of each other for a time prior to living near each other.

When I went back to Robinson High School, Tony and I became close. Soon after that, Grandma gave me the car that she had allowed it to sit for a while when it was not being used at all. The only thing I needed was my license. If I could just get my driver's license, I would be good to go. I would clean and wash my car regularly way before I could legally drive, just to get it ready. On my 16th birthday Kacky took me to take my test and get my license. You want to talk about a happy young man. Finally, the day I had been waiting for—it seemed like it took forever. Eric Folks being able to drive himself wherever, whenever, was such a great feeling. My parents were so laid back, allowing me to come and go as I pleased as long as I went to school and kept a job to keep a little money in my pocket for gas.

I had dreams for my car and how it could look if I could work at setting it up the way I wanted to. I was finally in the game. I had watched many people for many years with their nice rides, nice rims, windows tinted, stereo, lights, lowering, loud exhaust, etc. These are all things we do to make our cars look different from the factory look and I guess you could call it personalizing your ride. I was so ready and excited. No more riding the school bus either, how about that? Most of all we could cruise "the strip" Friday and Saturday nights.

8

THE STREETS, HOBBIES AND LESSONS

The strip was in Manassas and hundreds of people including us would hang there Friday and Saturday nights riding up and down Mathis Ave for hours. We would normally start around 8:00–9:00 p.m. and we would hang in the parking lots, in and out of 7-Eleven, restaurants, etc., until 12:00–1:00 a.m. We would go off and ride different streets and street race and all that. The police didn't like us hanging out, it just created a bunch of work for them; between the loud music, loud cars, rubber burning, street racing and drugs and alcohol (that I am sure took place) they really didn't want us hanging around there. So what else would they do beside put up a bunch of no loitering signs so they could give people tickets that led to fines for hanging out? They would set up roadblocks on this street to give us tickets to get us out of there. As you can imagine, a ton of people with nice cars who wanted every person to know what we had going on with our rides—we weren't going home. We would get our tickets and keep strolling around this area. It was kind of like the strip I had seen on *Boyz n the Hood* but without a lot of fighting and guns that was in the movie. Not to mention the police attention we received meant even more to the ladies watching for some. It was all part of that bad boy thing for most. For me it was really about the cars and hanging out and it was about the girls too, but not in a bad boy way, just us being who we were, and there wasn't anything else for us to do in Manassas VA, on a Friday or Saturday night for a lot of us.

It wasn't long after my cousin Thomas was driving his own ride and we were tight, I do mean tight. Wherever he was I was and wherever I was he was. You would have thought we were playing in the sand box once again with Tonka trucks just as we did when we were little kids. We would roll everywhere together. Most of all, Grandma's house was the place where we would do our construction. By construction I mean work on our cars. We would mastermind stereo work, work on other people's cars, and clean up our rides most of the time. I remember when it would rain, we didn't have a garage at her house so there was a parking garage nearby and we would go there to work on our cars just to stay out of the rain. If it was cold outside it didn't matter, if we had a mission, which was something to do, we would do it in the cold and all. I remember it being so cold outside we washed our cars and the water to rinse the vehicles would freeze, which included the tire shine when spraying it on the tires. My family loved a clean car and Thomas and I got that honestly from our family. We would spend all day cleaning up our cars and all night hanging out showing them off and following the groups of people and with that normally would include a lady or two to hang with. It wasn't long before I had my windows tinted, nice rims, lowered suspension, a loud exhaust and a loud stereo with subwoofers in the trunk. This was a completed master plan. I had turned Granny's car into a low rider, which a lot of people liked. Thomas and I would spend a lot of time at the car shops and hanging with other people with their cars.

I loved my car, I really did, there was only one problem; it was easy to keep clean and looked nice (at least to me), but my car was slow! It would do for the time being, but one of those days I was going to have a fast car (I said to myself). There were Honda Civics running turbos, escort GTs running glass packs, 240SXs with engine swaps, pickup trucks with hydraulics, and all. As you can see, I was appreciative of what I had, but it wasn't getting me any street credit other than being clean. It wasn't long after that when Aunt Kacky wanted to get rid of her 94 Dodge Shadow with the 3.0 v6 in it. Now this car was so fast for its time. A small car with a V6 and this thing would go really fast, I do mean fly (as in fast) in the compact car world. I don't know what the exact performance specs were, but this thing was an automatic and would burn the front tires up and pull to 100 mph quickly. I quickly said I wanted it. Well, I had had a few tickets for illegal equipment, which included fines, but they didn't go on my record. I would pay them and keep it moving without worrying about changing anything on the car, whether the car was too loud, too low, had neon lights, etc., but what I didn't realize was what speed really could or would do if something could or would go wrong while traveling at those speeds. You see I was a third-generation street gear head. My grandad "Pop" loved speed and my dad used to be an amazing street racer, per the stories I have heard now that I am older, so yeah, he was that guy. I think my dad knew this car was trouble, but I set my heart on it. It was clean as well. What did I do, become a clean street runner/racer with similar cars? Now, understand that this was different from the big V8 motors and the big boys, but I was more into the import world street racing, which is smaller engines but lighter cars that can go fast. So, I thought we would hit the strip, and then, when everyone got tired of that, we would ride over to DC (District of Columbia) to V Street.

We thought we were doing something riding up and down a street in Manassas. V Street was a scary scene, and I was way out of my league. My dad didn't want me going to DC and I didn't care for it, but when rolling with the crowd (which was rare for me), I would go every now and then. I got called out to run this guy and his nice Civic so I lined up to race and, just as we were going to take off, the police pulled up behind us and it scared me as I thought we would go to jail. V Street was a street that ran in between warehouses/storage units. The police were very aware that we were out there racing but wouldn't pull you over if you weren't racing. Even though we were lined up to take off they let us go. At the end of V Street there was a turn where you had to be slowed down enough to make it; if not, you could lose control of your car and crash. One time someone died while racing over there as they couldn't slow down fast enough to make the turn at the end from what the news said. So, just as we would run 100 mph on the highways to get over to V Street racing, we also did this on the way home. Needlessly to say, as I pushed the limit many times, it would only be a matter of time before I got caught just like everyone else.

One night, it was three of us on the way back home racing in and out of traffic, I thought I had seen a cop behind us; however, I was sure if it was a cop at the speeds we were running he would have pulled us over a long time ago. We continued to proceed with high speeds and just as we came around a curve on I-66 we saw another cop and both turned on their lights and pulled me and one of my boys over. Wow, here I was coming from DC where my dad told me not to go and I was being pulled over for running triple-digit speeds... I was on the side of the interstate with this state trooper very upset at 2:00 a.m. in the morning. I had only had my license for a few months. I was 16 with a ticket for reckless driving, exceeding the speed of 100 and racing. Wow, you want to talk about scared. I went home after the trooper let us go and woke my parents up and explained what I had done.

My dad was so mad. I worried about what would happen the next day once he got up. He was so mad at me he immediately had me take and give the Dodge Shadow back and get my 87 Stanza back because I had to drive to school daily. Most would ask why he didn't take my license and car. I was working and going to school away from where they lived so he allowed me to continue to drive for these reasons. Boy was I lucky, lucky that my dad didn't take my head off. This was huge and none of us knew the outcome of going to court. The only thing that would save me was that my boy who got the same ticket had a lawyer and just put a brand-new motor in his car. For those who don't know, when you put a new motor in a car, you are not supposed to run it very hard for break-in period or you can destroy the engine while running it hard. Between his new motor and lawyer (as we couldn't afford one and shouldn't have had to) they reduced it to improper driving... I am not sure how well that judge was feeling that day, but WOW I was lucky. I had to go with my dad to driving school, which was embarrassing, but I didn't have a fine or lose my license, which was a blessing. What a lesson learned for me. I would be lying if I told you I never did 100 plus mph again in my life. This was the time I learned a scary lesson.

While hanging out on the strip one night, like a normal weekend night, at the McDonald's, me and my friends were all in the parking lot and there were two older guys that walked by us and said something strange and I didn't quite catch what they said; I asked them who they were talking to. They immediately ran up to me and got all in my face and called me the "N word" and one said he had a gun in his back pocket and threatened to pull it out and shoot me dead right there. This was crazy because I looked around and a bunch of people I thought were my friends ran the other way. This was a life lesson to me. My dad once told me, "Son, you don't have any real friends." He said that years prior to this moment; I didn't know what he meant at the time, but I would soon find out. As these two men that are in their 40s it appeared I was a bit scared because they were so grownup, and I was a young kid and didn't want to fight them in case I lost, and they really had a gun. Someone heard the word "gun" and called the police; as they went on yelling at me, a car came into the McDonald's parking lot from the exit side—not the entrance—and the car slid sideways and this big guy got out of the car and the two guys started running. Right beside the parking lot was a trailer park. The big guy started chasing them as they ran. We chased them into the trailers and they ended up going into one of them. As we are leaving to come back to our cars, I didn't know the other guy at all, the cops were there because they were called about a gun; they pulled their guns out on us and made us get on the ground. This was the first time I had a gun drawn on me ever and there were multiple police. They were doing their job, but man how scary. After looking at this, to see two guys come out of the woods I am sure they had to take precautions. Here I was on the ground in handcuffs waiting for the story to be cleared. This was my very first time in the back of a police car as well and hopefully it would be my last forever. One of the other people came out and got it straight after they searched us and put us in the back of their car. Eventually they let us go. This was the first time I had been directly involved in a racist issue with a grownup. It was a crazy experience and scary all at the same time. Come to find out the same guy who drove the car into the parking lot sliding sideways got in a fight with them and their buddies at a local pool hall. He had knocked their friend's teeth out with a cue ball. That is why they were so upset at any black person they could find; it just so happened to be me. This was just one of those crazy nights on the strip.

While living in Westgate I met a guy named Sam. Sam was the man, later I would find out just how cool he was. He had two boys and lived together with his kid's mom. Sam drove a BMW coupe and really had his stuff together. He was much older than me in age. He worked hard and never seemed to sweat anything and had no problems telling someone what was on his mind or calling someone out for saying something crazy. Sam quickly became a role model for me as we hung out like we were family. He never let the age difference between us seem weird or anything. He treated me like a son but an equal at the same time. We would hang out and ride out together. I remember one time he let me drive his BMW to the store and I couldn't figure out how to get it into reverse. BMWs have a different gear pattern for reverse than most cars I had ever driven. Sam was making good money as I could tell, and I picked up a lot of wisdom from him. He really seemed to have his stuff together. We would hang with our other friends and go to DC late at night and get subs to eat and have drinks. DC restaurants late-night window pickup had the best subs and they would be very large compared to other restaurants I was used to. I was always a big guy and could eat, but these subs I could only eat like one portion and have the rest for later, it was awesome.

I remember one time I was so down because my front bumper on my Stanza got messed up and cracked in half and I didn't have the money to have it repaired. Sam helped me take it off and showed me how to glue it back together. It wasn't pretty, but it was back together. For him to take his time and help me was touching. When he sold his BMW, he gave me the stereo speakers out of it and asked nothing in return. It may seem simple to some, but people did not do this on a regular basis where we grew up. Most people did as much as they could to get money out of whatever they had to sell and not give it away. Sam was a true inspiration and a brother to me, and I am grateful for him showing me many things in life. I still look up to him to this day.

9

INTRO TO GIRLS
AND WOMEN

A round this time is when the girls really started to heat up and I was in my teenage years. I mean I had girlfriends way before this point in my life, but things started to get deeper. When I was younger, I had a few girls (at the time) in my life that made a big impact on me either at that time or later as I looked back. It is amazing how when we are young, we don't really know what we want in life so there is no way we can know who we want. Later I learned this and will explain it as the story continues. My grandma had a neighbor who was a friend and they had been neighbors for years. I remember Grandma would borrow money from him from time to time to make sure she had what she needed as she took care of so many. He would look out for her when she asked. He had two granddaughters that I knew directly. One was older than the other. When I was young, about 14 years old, I started talking with one of them as we all played together—herself, me, my cousins—whenever I would come around. She was fun to hang around and was the young wild girl. She would buy me things and give me money and, truth be told, for a young boy this seemed like an awesome friendship to have. We were more than friends but without any kind of commitment to each other, which was kind of strange, but it was the way we decided to leave it until we got tired of it. We talked on and off for a couple of years. Eventually I started talking to her older cousin. She was a good girl and she was crazy about me. She really would do just about anything for me. She was already out of school while I was still in school, she had a job and all. She was one of those women who really wanted the best for me, and I truly didn't understand it. I couldn't understand it. I found out later in life how much she really liked and cared for me and would have done almost anything for me and I was blind to it at the time. This is important and the reason why is because life taught me many lessons later on about relationships. It was tough at the time to know what I wanted. There were times I wanted to act older and mature and then I had moments when I wanted to be young, wild and careless. I learned "you can't have your cake and eat it too," that is a saying that many older people would say when I was younger.

When I was around 15 years old, I met a young lady named Katie. She was the daughter of a friend of my uncle Tony's. Katie's dad and Tony worked together, and I met her at a company function one time. When I met her, there was something special about her. At a later time we reconnected. Katie had a son. He was a baby when we linked up; however, I immediately fell in love with him. He was a special baby I could tell. Katie was a nice young girl and I fell for her very quickly. I would look out for her as much as I could. You see I was that "nice guy" that a lot of the girls didn't like in the younger days. I would show up on dates with roses and that wasn't always a great first impression for a young girl. Their moms seemed to appreciate it but not them. Most of them liked the bad boy style guys. By bad boy, I mean those that are in the streets getting into trouble, being disrespectful, the kind of guys that would treat them wrong in the long run, but they couldn't see it. Life is wild how we can want something today that doesn't have a lot of promise for the future at that moment. I wasn't that guy. I refused to be that guy as it wasn't in my nature or character. Katie and I dated for a while and ended up breaking up after some time. I liked her a lot and thought maybe she was the one I would spend many years with in life, but we couldn't connect on a few things. She was young and of course so was I; however, I felt so strongly about her and our future. I didn't mind that she had a child at such a young age. I still would check in on them from time to time to see how they were doing and felt that we could possibly get back together at some point, but I would let her go live her life. Later in my life she did try to come back into the picture, but it was way late for that.

Being the young guy I was, I moved on. One night, while hanging on the strip, I met a nice lady named Marcy. Marcy was nice and was a bit older than me; she was around 23 and I was 17 at the time. Marcy and I spent some time together. She had a daughter when we met who was around three at the time. Marcy was such a sweetheart. We would spend a lot of our time together at weekends. She met my parents and they liked her as well. It was exciting dating her and with her being older she carried herself way different than any other girls I had dated. She was sweet, kind and very loving. There came a time when I got scared of having a future with Marcy because of how much older she was and her having a daughter. We got along very well, but I was afraid I wouldn't be able to live my life as I truly wanted to. Naturally what normally happens when a young boy gets scared of a woman? Notice I said boy and she was clearly a woman and I wasn't ready for her. So, I messed it up. Katie had started calling me again and found out that I was dating someone else. I didn't want to be locked down at this time with a lot of responsibilities, so I broke up with Marcy and got back with Katie.

Looking back at this I learned a valuable lesson. Sometimes people just want you to make sure no one else has you. That is what Katie did and I fell for the trap and broke Marcy's heart. I can still remember the conversation to break up with her and how I felt just breaking her heart. She was really in love with me, she truly was, and I messed that up big time.

I believe in my life there have been very few women who truly wanted the best for me and loved me for all of who I was. Marcy was super special and still is in a very respectful way. I would run into her from time to time and there was so much respect for our past between us. She would ask about my mom and family.

So, I decided to take Katie to the prom. After breaking up with Marcy, I wasn't big into the prom and school functions; however, we did go and it was a great time. We spent the entire night out together partying and all. It wasn't long after that we stopped talking again. I found out later that she was going out with one of my cousins. This wasn't the first time this happened where he or I would start talking with each other's ex. We didn't make a habit of it or try to do it. Being young and hanging out in the same areas all the time it just happened this way sometimes. This time it was different, it was a little painful. Katie wasn't just some girl in my life, she was one of the special women that I had been with at the time and although we didn't talk anymore, she was that one. My cousin and I didn't fight over her or anything as I had long moved on, it was just a sensitive situation not to mention weird for a change. My feelings were hurt, but I also understood the game we played back then.

10

STAY HUMBLE

I started my first real job in the automotive field when I was around 17. I got the job through school. This is where my experience in business really started. I knew someone like me, who didn't really understand school, would have to put in work if I was ever going to be successful because I wouldn't have a college degree in the work field. What better business to be in than with the cars that I loved so much? It was time for me to learn what working in an automotive shop was all about and start to deal with management on a regular basis. Now, this job was different than others because the automotive field is a tough field and there are times when the pressures of sales, production and teammates just don't line up and management has to figure out what to do and how to do it to still meet goals and maximize performance. I am not saying this to say any other business aren't the same; however, I worked fast food and if people showed up for a burger then that is what they got. In the automotive business someone could show up for a $19.00 oil change and only in express lube businesses do oil changes keep the doors open. I started off as a general service tech. I was the guy who changed the oil in cars, changed the tires and kept the shop straight for Merchant's Tire and Auto in Woodbridge, VA. We had deals we had to meet; there was nothing like a vehicle pulling into the shop and we had a guarantee of installing four tires within 30 minutes or less depending on your style of wheels or fast oil changes. You want to talk about getting burned? Try draining oil out of a vehicle that just got finished being in a rush to meet a 30-minute window. These were some of the challenges we faced as techs and I loved the challenge. It was like a race, a race against the clock and time.

My school counselor helped me get the job with some connection they had. This is where I met Nick Marshall. Nick was a guy who I found later was a good guy; he didn't take no mess when it came to business. He was the assistant manager and he was one of those assistant managers that really did the job of the main manager while the main manager did whatever—that is how it appeared anyway. Nick was the guy there from open to close answering all the questions whenever they came up most of the time. He was a great boss and we became friends as he did with a lot of his techs. I didn't realize how much I was learning from him at the time and how I could apply it later in my career really for a lifetime. He had and still does to this day a great work ethic and a passion for others. I am so grateful to him and his abilities not only to lead by example but to help me throughout the beginning of my career. Sometimes in life we meet people and they really help us take off in more than one way in our life. Nick loved hockey, jet skis and motorcycles. I worked very hard to do my job to the best of my abilities.

There was a position that came up after I turned 18 and graduated and it was for retail sales manager. I wanted this position so bad and Nick and I talked about it. He also thought it would be a great position for me. Unfortunately, it wasn't solely up to him and me. After applying and Nick co-signing the promotion, I learned a very valuable lesson in the politics of the workplace. Another guy who didn't even work for the company got the position. Nick wasn't happy about it and neither was I. I had two choices here. I could get bitter about the situation or I could look deeper at the situation to find out why I wasn't selected for the position. I looked deep into the situation and I couldn't see any reason outside of lack of experience. If I didn't have experience how was I ever going to get it if they didn't give me the chance? This was the question I had. This is what is amazing about God; sometimes it may seem that I am being overlooked and He's maybe just showing others a lesson. The new guy they hired instead of me ended up working for a short amount of time, he only lasted a few days and quit and never came back.

Here was my chance again. I knew if I had been salty and showed an ugly side of my personality, they would never have reconsidered me for the position. With Nick's confidence and push for me they ended up promoting me from the shop to the office. I was so happy and knew that being in this business was something that could take me to the next level. I had so much to learn. This wasn't an easy position to handle. I was barely out of school and having to manage guys who were as old as my parents was a scary thought. Nick was a great coach and always had my back no matter what; it made a huge difference in my life and how I performed as a part of the management team. Here I was a young man with management on my resume. As much as I loved cars, I knew that working in the office was a great fit for me rather than working on cars directly.

While I worked at Merchants Tire and went to school things got tougher in school due to my lack of concentration and even wanting to apply myself. There came a point in school where I realized that, even when I applied myself, I still struggled very badly. I had to ask myself if I had a learning disability. Maybe all this time I was skipping school acting up, which wasn't my personality, and possibly this was my way of covering up a problem that I had. It wasn't uncommon for people to struggle to learn. I realized I could duplicate a lot by visually see-ing someone do it; reading it, remembering it and applying it was a real struggle. After failing classes in high school, I knew I couldn't give up. There were a lot of people in my family who didn't graduate high school—my parents didn't, my brothers and some aunts and uncles—but I had to no matter what. I real-ized how important this was not only for my family but for my-self, but it was late when I started to apply myself. I opened up and talked with my counselor about my struggles and needed to go through testing to find out if I did have a learning disability and what options I had moving forward. All this time I avoided applying myself due to fear of failing even when I tried my best, and instead of finding out why, I simply blew it off and here I was in the last few years of school finding out. Wow, if I would have applied myself better, I could have gotten the help I needed earlier in life and could have had a different view on school. I ended up taking the same subjects; however, the classes were re-duced-size classes where I could get the attention and help I needed to learn and really take my time to learn. It is amazing the difference that made for me.

If there is anyone out there struggling with school, I encour-age you to ask for help and continue asking until you get the help you need.

I had failed so many classes I not only had to continue going to school during the day, I had to take a couple of night classes and work. It wasn't easy, but I made it by the grace of God and that is all that mattered at the time.

In June of 1997, I graduated from Robinson High School. It was such a proud moment for me and my family. I couldn't believe it; we finally made it. I say we as I was the first to graduate in my immediate family and the joy that came with it was amazing. I believe this was one of the proudest moments in my life that I had with my parents and family. We took pictures and went out to dinner; it was an awesome moment in my life. Instead of going to beach week with all my friends, I continued to work to make sure I had the money to get by and live. I felt like I missed out on a lot at this time in my life, but little did I know I was building my work ethic, and this would help me stay focused on my goals later in life. You may be at a point where you feel you are missing out on a party or things of that nature. What seemed to be important then is not important now. I didn't miss out on anything at that time.

I worked for Merchants for a while after that. I remember my first big repair ticket that I sold to a customer. You see the way that it worked is that customers would come in for regular service, an oil change or something like that, and then we had to look over their vehicle to see if it needed anything else and then up sale them the remaining items. The vehicle was a Mazda 626; I can remember it like it was yesterday. The technician came in with a list of things that he recommended on the vehicle that were needed for maintenance, which included all four tires, suspension struts, wheel alignment, etc. Normally Nick would handle something like this, but it was my time to learn. I had watched him do it a bunch of times and it was my turn. I was nervous going up to this customer to sale them seven hundred dollars' additional worth of work give or take. I sat down beside them and stuttered and stumbled through my entire conversation with this customer and they said yes! I was so excited and from there it was a bit easier to speak with customers. After all, customers are people who need to feel that you care and you aren't out just to get their money. It is about trust and relationships. If a customer trusts you, they will trust what you have to say to them and why.

While living in Woodbridge I learned quite a few life lessons. I used to hang out with a neighbor; he was a few years older than me. Hammer is what we called him; he was a cool guy (at the time I thought). It is amazing how I grew up thinking someone was cool and later in life I realized that simply knowing someone could have cost me my life by the choices I made and being associated with them. The Bible tells us that bad company corrupts good character. I do know that Hammer and the neighbors used to party quite often, which included drinking and smoking different substances. Women would hang over there and it seemed like the place to be. One weekend, Hammer got into it at a club with some local people who had street influence and he needed to make a run down to the southern VA area as he had some connections to some people who were into dealing drugs and gangs. Hammer asked me if I wanted to ride, it was on a weekend and I figured why not, what could it hurt? Little did I know it could hurt a lot. The plan was to go down there and for him to get some protection for the streets and come back the same night. Well, on the way there we were drinking a little bit (yes, I was underage)—first mistake—and smoking some stuff also. We got there and picked up what we needed to. Truth be told, I thought he was picking up a handgun, but it turns out he was picking up much more than a handgun, which didn't fit in the trunk with all the stereo equipment he had in his ride. We had to lay the backseat down with the guns wrapped in a blanket; you couldn't tell what it was, but you could still see it from the inside of the car. I didn't know anything about guns other than what I had seen on TV. One thing I did know was street code, you don't ask, and they won't tell. They won't tell even if you ask, so don't ask what the guns were used for.

Hammer wanted to stop a few streets over from the main strip at VA beach on the way back home. I hadn't been on the strip at night before, so I was good with it. I had never even been to a beach in my life at this point. He had an ex-girlfriend that lived there. We stopped by her house and they wanted to hang out together prior to us heading back home. I wanted to go hang on the main strip at the beach. I asked if it was cool if I used the car. He said yes it was cool. I went out and got in the car and went to pull off and looked back (Lord have mercy, God was looking out for me) and saw the blankets with guns wrapped in there. So, I thought it was a good idea to take the guns out of the car in case I got pulled over (I was famous for getting pulled over when driving cars that got attention of others). So, I took the guns into the house and went on toward the strip. I wasn't on the strip for a few minutes before I got pulled over. WOW was this scary… I got pulled over for loud music (on the beach front strip) are you kidding me? The car didn't have a front tag (illegal in VA) on the car I was driving (his car). Here I was in the middle of the main strip in VA beach away from home. No front tag, loud music and I didn't want to dig too deep around the car because I didn't know what I would find. This is where God's grace went deeper to help me out of this situation that I was clearly in deep waters with. I didn't know Hammer's real name; the car wasn't even registered to him. It was registered in the name of someone who was in prison. I just knew I was in hot water and going to jail. To think if I didn't get those guns out of the car, I would have gone to jail for many, many, many years. I could still be in jail today depending on the status of the gun, clean or dirty. I would put money on it that it was dirty.

The police officer looked in the car and said, "I see you have the keys so you must've gotten permission to drive the vehicle. If it comes up stolen, I know where to find you." He wrote me tickets and let me go. You want to talk about God's grace and mercy saving me this day, wrong place at the wrong time, with the wrong people, associated with something I had no business being associated with. Sometimes we pray to God to just get us out of a mess that we got ourselves into and this was one of those times. I immediately left the strip and picked up Hammer and we headed back home. Picture this, my first time at a beach was 10 mins (three tickets), almost jail time probably for life, based on some very bad decisions I made.

On the way back home, because we had been drinking and smoking (way early in the day) the sleepiness started to set in and as I was driving, and Hammer was sleeping, I fell asleep driving 80 plus mph. As the car drifted off the road the highway had the safety divots in it designed to wake anyone up driving and running off the road. This happened twice on this trip home prior to me knowing I couldn't drive any more. (I wasn't drunk at all and hadn't drank in hours but was exhausted from being up all day and the trip, not to mention the activity earlier) Hammer ended up waking up as we both did, and he drove the rest of the drive home. As I looked back on that day, I was grateful to God for saving me for making such poor decisions. This part of my life is called grace… Eventually Hammer was arrested for his past issues that happened to catch up with him again with the bounty hunters and I never saw him again.

11

FROM CITY LIFE TO COUNTRY LIFE

My parents ended up moving from Woodbridge to Fluvanna County, which is about 120 miles away from where we were they were still in Virginia. I ended up moving with my grandma again and her house was already full, so I slept on the floor, with a sleeping bag of course, for a while. I wasn't anywhere ready to live on my own. This was an example of my grandma's generosity. She may not have had a room for me or anyone else, but we could always crash on her floor. Her house was like a safe house for us all. It didn't matter who it was, if you needed a roof over your head, she would allow it. Writing this makes me smile and think of her. She was so selfless, always looking out for others, especially her family. I stayed with her for a while and then ended up moving in with my brother Mike and his longtime girlfriend at the time Robin. Robin was the nicest, she always looked out to make sure I had food to eat and things like that. She is such a nice lady. She had been with Mike since I was in middle school.

While in high school Robin was at home taking care of their son Damian, my nephew. I would go by their house and play around with Damian on the floor and mess around with him and she would always offer me food and help me out so I wouldn't go hungry. Eating was not a problem for me, and she knew it. I would get big plates of macaroni and cheese. Robin could cook quite well. I ended up moving in with them for a while as I was working and hanging out trying to figure out what was next in my life. Mike and Robin's house was the place to be, they always had cookouts and parties at their spot. The corner of Manassas Drive and Route 28 in Manassas (right near the strip) is where they lived. We would sit out and all my friends that I had known from years would drive past and show some love with their cars beeping their horns, while playing loud music and doing burnouts right in the middle of the road (as long as the police weren't around). No matter how much fun it was staying there I missed my parents very much as I didn't see them that much due to me working a lot and hanging out at other times with friends.

I eventually moved to Fluvanna with my parents. We had been close, and truth be told, I wasn't ready to be away from them like that. I was working for Graybar Electric at this time. That was the company Robin worked at for years (she had gotten me a job there) and they had a branch in Richmond. I ended up transferring to their Richmond branch. Fluvanna was really country; I mean really country, the entire county I think had one traffic light in it. Maybe two, but you get the point. It was different living so far away from the city. The closest city was Charlottesville. Fluvanna was quiet though and for the first time I could sit outside and not hear any cars, any neighbors, any anything for hours. It was good but scary at the same time. I say scary because I was so used to seeing people and being able to hang out and have a great time. Charlottesville was a way away, about 25 miles give or take, and I was used to hanging out on the strip on the weekends but there was no strip, it was so different. They had areas to hang out but nothing like I was used to.

Working at Graybar in Richmond was fun and tough, I was a warehouse worker and although it was the same thing I was doing in northern VA, the atmosphere was different. My favorite part about working there was cutting wire. We had to use a fork-lift to lift these big spools of wire and we would have to reel them from one spool to the other depending on how much was needed for the customer's order. It was dangerous but challenging as well. It was different in many ways; I met a few people there. We would work very hard cutting wire and spooling it.

There were a bunch of people that worked in the warehouse. It was about an hour's ride from our house we lived in. I was used to an hour's ride but not through the woods and all that mileage. Some days it was just hard to stay awake while driving with no traffic lights, straight highway.

I didn't spend any time in Richmond; I really didn't like the area. Richmond reminded me of DC in a lot of ways, lots of traffic, people everywhere and the streets were rough. Not streets as in danger but big potholes and things that the city life brings. Although we used to go to V Street, I didn't hang out in DC outside of that. I didn't like to hang out there or anything. I went to work and back out of the Richmond area. I didn't take time to understand or explore the different areas of Richmond. This is something that I learned later in life; that it is important that we take time to explore. If we don't like something maybe it is because it is different and we haven't given ourselves enough time to really see the positives of things.

While working in Richmond I met a guy named "Big Man", we called him that; I am not sure what his real name is. He was a big dude, probably 6 foot 5 inches and over 300 pounds, and was cool; he called me "ERIE". He was the type of guy you could tell anything. No matter how tough things were he would have the coolest attitude. In the short time that I knew him he was fun to be around, and we would share stories. I also met a young lady named Samantha, she was also one of those blessings (that appeared to have fallen from the sky) and I had no idea of the connection we would make or the impact she would have on my life at a later time. I am talking years later I realized this.

Samantha was familiar with Robin over the phone as they would communicate every now and then for work from branch to branch with Graybar. Samantha and I ended up linking up from seeing each other. She was nice and kind. We would sit outside and chat at lunch; Big Man used to make little jokes like "Here come your girl, Erie." It used to make me smile. Samantha and I ended up hanging out outside of work. She had her own place near work, the first lady as an adult I ever dated that had their own place. We would do things like go to the movies, listen to music, hang at her house, and she would cook dinner for us. We would hang out and chill while talking about life. I remember one of the cutest times of us hanging out. She wanted to drive my car, but she couldn't drive a manual 5 speed that well. I was in her car a few cars ahead of her and she couldn't get the car going properly and we had to switch cars in the middle of traffic. It was so funny and cute at the same time. We laughed and giggled about that....Samantha was one of the first women to really treat me like a man as I met her after I was the age of 18. What I mean by that is she respected me as the man I was and didn't look at me for who I wasn't. When she looked at me it meant something. I just couldn't understand what that look was at the time. I was young, and, truth be told, I didn't know what that could be or how important it was. She would talk on the phone to her mom and mention me as they would chat. She also met my mom, my dad and my sister and they were familiar with her. When I think back about what we had growing, it makes me smile. We had good times hanging out and always had great conversations.

I stayed at her house a few times overnight, she loved cars also. Her dad had taught her how to work on her own cars. Big Man would ask me when I stayed over, "Erie, what sup with you and ole girl, Erie!" I still smile today just thinking about it. Like the relationship I had with Marcy, I wasn't ready, and truth be told, I was afraid of Samantha and what we could be. I was still chasing some things and seeking some things but I had no idea of what they were. I was so used to moving around and I wasn't ready at this moment of my life to be committed to a relationship. I ended up leaving Graybar and going back to work for Merchant's Tire in a very small town called Waynesboro that I had never been to. This was 50 miles in the opposite direction of Richmond from Fluvanna and, needless to say, Samantha and I stopped talking over time. As I look back, I believe God puts people in our lives for a reason and some for a season. Sometimes

I believe it is the blessing we need and depending on how we think about that blessing or are thankful for the blessing, God will allow them to move out of our lives. I know today that Samantha was a true blessing and they say opposites attract. I do believe that, but I don't think long-term opposites make the best relationships. You will read about that more as the book continues.

12

EVERYTHING CHANGED

This was my first time being in Waynesboro. For those that don't know Waynesboro is outside of Charlottesville, which is in the mountains in the valley in Central Virginia. It is a pretty place to look at from outside of the town with all the mountains. It is a very small town. I went to work back for Merchant's Tire in Waynesboro. I didn't spend much time in Waynesboro, I drove there to work and left for home daily. The ride was quite the distance, just as it was in Richmond, but the same distance in the opposite direction. The only good thing about the ride was I had to go past Charlottesville and I could always stop in the city and hang out a little while to break up the drive.

One day, I was in the customer lounge at Merchants while working looking at the TV and the lounge was surrounded by glass and I noticed a young lady across the street. I didn't think much about it after that. Little did I know that one day this would be the lady I would marry, love and have a family with. One day, I was at a traffic light waiting to go get lunch and that same young lady was sitting at the red light beside me and we caught eye contact for a moment until the light turned and I proceeded. I thought to myself, *That is the same girl I saw at the gas station that day I was watching TV.* A couple of days went by and, one day, while I was working, I answered the phone and a young lady said she wanted to price tires. This wasn't unusual for me; after all, I sold tires for a living. This young lady was different for some reason and then she asked me if I was the new guy in town. That goes to show you how small this town is; however, it was her. I had no idea this day would change my life forever.

We exchanged information and began to talk to each other over the phone. As we got to know each other I found that she was born and raised in the town of Waynesboro. She had a ton of family in this town also. She was a few years older than me, she was 23 and I was 19 at the time. She was very interesting that I found, and she was different from the girls I had dated in the past. We talked for a while and started seeing each other on a regular basis, we would go to the park on my lunch time and things like that. It was funny when we would go to the park on lunch breaks, the geese would chase her and she would jump on my back to get away from them. She had two boys that were twins. They were three years old at the time I met Tracy. Justice and Justin. They were the cutest little boys. They really were. I remember the first time I met them. Tracy and the boys lived with Tracy's mom Judy. Tracy worked a part-time job while being a single mother. The twins' dad was around, however not too often. The family had an amazing love for the twins Justice and Justin. I continued to live in Fluvanna and drive to Waynesboro. Tracy's mom Judy worked at night so from time to time I would stay in Waynesboro. It was nice not having to drive home all the time. Most of Tracy's family was tight back then as in they would come around to see each other often. I found that Tracy was really close with her grandparents who lived around the corner from her and her mom. It wasn't long before Tracy met my parents and I met most of her family.

As time went on Tracy and I spent more time together. I found out that her dad wasn't in her life much growing up. It appears he would come around every now and then but not too often. There were even stories of whether he claimed her as his daughter. Tracy's real dad (the man who raised her) was her grandad (Paul Diggs). She looked up to him in ways that I haven't seen a child look up to their grandparent. I could tell right away that there was a special bond between them and that she looked at him as a dad.

Paul was a special man; he really was in many ways. I learned so much from him in the short amount of years that we spent together on and off. I was young back then and reserved. I didn't talk a lot; however, I always listened that was for sure. As we all spent time together, I could tell that Tracy had grown up in an environment that most of us wish we had, surrounded by love and support. Her grandad was her dad. She had a few uncles that she really looked up to. The Diggs family was tight. My family was tight also but not this tight. As we grew up our family grew apart, but this family was still tight even with the adults and children. Watching Paul, I learned a very valuable lesson about how a father gets older and the respect for him and the love got deeper as time went on. He was truly the head of his family. Kind of like a king of a castle and honored as such. There could be an argument going on or something of that nature and he could shut it down simply by speaking to let everyone know to let it go. This was so different from the family I had seen growing up, as I explained earlier in this book the love from my dad's side of the family was the complete opposite. The respect wasn't there. I can clearly see the difference as I look back.

It wasn't long after Tracy and I met that we moved in together. Although we could have easily moved into my parents' place with them as they had the space, I was ready to move out on my own. My parents were okay with whatever I wanted to do as it was my decision. They would never pressure to stay or to go. It would have been nice to stay, but they lived so far away, and it just made sense to get our own place. Judy was good with us moving. She didn't care for the fact that I would stay in her house from time to time, it only made sense as Tracy and I weren't married. She had voiced her opinion on that and out of respect it was the right thing to do. We moved into our own apartment. Wow, here I was out of the house at 19 years old and with my own little family. I didn't understand what was going on at the time or the impact I could have on the twins and everyone around me. It seemed as I was going with the flow of life. This is what I had learned from the people around me including my dad. We had a two-bedroom apartment and I was off to officially being an adult. I learned something in life, age doesn't make you an adult by any means. Most people think that once you are 18 years old you are automatically an adult, how wrong we are. It is simply the age you can be on your own and legally responsible for every move you make.

There were times I didn't feel that Judy (Tracy's mom) cared for me much; however, I had learned growing up that everyone isn't going to like me or everything that I do. I knew I was a good guy and knew that over time she would really get to know who I was. I do not want to speak for her, and we never discussed it; however, I viewed it as a city boy coming to the town of Waynesboro with my loud music, flashy rims and outgoing attitude it sometimes takes time to adjust to. Many may have saw me as cocky or arrogant, it was simply a confidence that I had developed over the years as there was many that didn't care for me. It was just the way life was growing up. Very strange though, most moms of the girls I dated loved me, but this time it was different. Little did I know that one day we would have an amazing relationship and share much love for our family and for each other. The way I viewed this was just that, my view, which was as we grow, we often change the way we look at things. I don't blame her for not knowing my angle, it was my place to prove my character. I know I was up to only good and over time I hoped she would see it. In life a lot of times we who are the softest have to put up a wall. At least that is what I thought way back then.

It wasn't long after being in our own place that Tracy and I would have our very first "big fight", being young and not visiting the basics of relationships (I will get into that more later) it was going to happen and when it did, I wouldn't know how to handle it as I should have. So here it is: BOOM we get into our first major argument, which a lot of relationships have. Where I came from this isn't something that I should have to deal with, and her view was whatever also. When two people aren't focused on the outcome of the solution, what happens? A messy situation becomes even messier. Here we are, we are arguing and fussing with each other and I get so mad that I decide to cut a phone cord. I don't even remember what the argument was about; however, what I do know is that is a super red flag because anger isn't in my character, especially mad enough to cut a cord I would have to replace with a new one. I don't remember the reason for the argument as I said, but instead of me looking into that (much later I life I learned about character) I left and tried to talk to Tracy's female friends. This is a huge no-no, which we all know, but again I didn't care. It wasn't that I was trying to get even with Tracy, it was that I have always been taught if you want to be here then be here; if not, it's time to move on. Little did I know she had a little game of her own going on with her ex at the time. I found this out later; when we had yet another argument, she threw it in my face. It isn't unusual for people in the heat of the moment to throw pain at someone they want to get back at. This was another red flag on both of our ends now that I look back on it.

I found that Merchant's would be closing the location I was at some time in the future and although I loved living less than five minutes away from my job, things had got complicated between Tracy and me and I'd had enough of the town (at the time) so my boy (from childhood) Tony Harris was working for a government contactor back in northern VA and they had additional openings, so I decided to go back to northern VA and leave Waynesboro. It felt good to be back up in northern VA, where I grew up, I was staying with my grandma again at the time and as always, just as she was there for everyone, she was there for me, providing a place to stay and that grandma love that only a grandma can provide. I found myself reconnecting with some of my old friends, hanging out having a good time. It wasn't long after that I found I was missing Tracy in a big way and thought to myself, *I wonder what life would be like if she moved to northern VA with me.* Robin had spoken to me about me missing her. I guess she could read it in my spirit or something, but she was right. Tracy had talked about how it would be living in the city, but I also knew how tight she was with her family. I really didn't know if she would move or not. I asked her to move away from her family and come up with me. She agreed. Now, notice that I didn't mention anything about how we worked out our problems or anything of that sort. Looking back this is a problem and a common mistake that we make in relationships thinking that time fixed things only to find out that time didn't fix anything because it doesn't work that way. Time doesn't heal all wounds as some would think.

We agreed that she would move in with me and the twins would stay with her family and we would work and get a place of our own and the twins would move in with us later. This is another mistake that we made, something I didn't realize at this time is even though we struggled in a major way as a family growing up, we did just that—we stayed as a family and that is the way it should be. It wasn't that we abandoned the twins; it is just that they should have stayed under our roof even though we all agreed it was best for them to stay with Tracy's grandparents and her Mom. We knew they would be taken great care of, that was never in question and that is what made it so easy and convenient to decide on. We ended up getting a place in Woodbridge with my brother Derrick and his friend. Our neighbors were an old co-worker from Merchant's. We used to party and I do mean party hard. While living here I turned 21 and we would have such a great time, either going out to bars or partying at our houses. Either way there was always a party going on. There were days we didn't remember all the details of the night before because we partied so hard. We would go to Waynesboro quite often to see the twins; Tracy seemed to be going there every couple of weeks and spending the weekend. Really spending time with her family. I was so in the zone of my own, I couldn't see the importance of this. I couldn't put my finger on it; however, it was as if I was being so selfish I didn't think about the bond that I should have been building. We would send money and I would help when I could, but that truly wasn't good enough. It really wasn't and there is no excuse for my actions in my life back then.

It was around this time I had a big scare. A young lady I used to talk with and hang out with reached out to me through a friend to reconnect with me. I guess she had heard Tracy and I were together, not knowing Tracy, but remembering me. I didn't have any interest at this time to talked with her, and I was informed by her that I had a daughter. For me this was a big deal as it would be or should be for anyone out there in the world. I stopped by her place one day to talk with her and meet this beautiful little girl. As I met her the timing that we were hanging out added up in the years. There was something missing though, in my heart of hearts I had to ask why this wasn't shared with me prior and why then. Weeks went by and we had a serious talk and come to find out she wasn't my daughter as the young lady was trying to get attention from me and admitted what she was trying to do. It was a scary thought to think, this really could happen, and I am sure does happen to people frequently. It was scary and sad while some people will do this for attention and what could have happened if I fell for the trap.

By now I had left the contracting company I was working for and decided to get into cable TV working as a technician. I loved to troubleshoot, so this job fit me. It wasn't an easy job by any means being out in the rain all day, sometimes snow, in house attics at 100 degrees. There were some really tough days, but I have never been afraid of hard work and continued to work through it just knowing one day I would find the next thing. That is something I learned from my dad, although he worked a lot of jobs, and I do mean a lot, he always told me to learn as much as I can while I can. He said you never know when you must fall back onto something that you have done in the past. Although I never understood why he worked so many jobs, this did make sense to me. It made good sense and probably some of the best advice my dad has given me in this lifetime.

I went from one cable company to another. While working for Comcast I made some great connections. One of them being becoming great friends with Daniel Bostick. I learned a lot from Daniel about friendship, family, loyalty. At the time I didn't know that we would become long-time brothers. He is the type of guy who has no problems saying exactly what is on his mind. He also was one of the first people that I met who really wasn't afraid of much of anything. I do mean anything… If there was a problem on my end he had no problem jumping in there having my back 100% all the time. He met my family and I met his. He was a family member and that was real. He even calls my mother Mom. He would come to family cookouts and all. He was down for me and I was down for him. We were true brothers outside of blood. I hadn't met anyone who showed me this kind of loyalty, love and friendship in all my life to be honest. Daniel would take a bullet for me and I would take one for him, it was that simple.

I remember once we were in a bar and some guy was talking trash, Daniel is short in height and this guy was tall. Daniel stood up on a bar stool to hit the guy on the head with a bottle, but he was stopped prior to fighting the guy. He didn't play around when it came to handling his business in a physical way. Daniel was the first one to teach me to shoot a gun and he also carried a gun as a concealed weapon.

Around this time in my life Tracy was pregnant with our first child together, Trey. This was very exciting to me. There was nothing more important to me than to be a good father to my child. I always had said growing up that I planned to marry the woman I had children with, and I had never wanted to have children by multiple women if things didn't work out. I also know today looking back that is a great thought and the way it should be, what I didn't think of is that if I was all in and would do whatever it took to make it work, that commitment may just get me into some things that I didn't want to be in. Here I was, baby on the way, committed to being a great father, only one thing left to do. That was get married. Again, here we were, I had great intentions but no clue what the commitment of marriage meant. This is where life would start to teach me not to be so anxious about making decisions that could affect me or others for a lifetime. I still had plenty of female friends that I kept in touch with. I didn't do this to cheat or anything of that nature, I had lived in the same area all my life and it wasn't anything to stay in touch. After all, I didn't have "bad breakups" with girl-friends in the past. It would always be a discussion and agree-ment and nine out of 10 times we would remain friends.

Tracy and I decided after long discussions that we would get married. The pressure to get married was heavy, there is no ques-tion. Tracy struggled with the fact of our child having my last name without being married as well and the twins didn't have their dad's last name. This was another major concern, as you have read there were a lot of issues that were huge that we ig-nored and pushed through and this was one of them. You see, when I was born, I had my mom's ex-husband's last name, which is my brother's last name, Nicholson. I don't have a prob-lem with the last name, but it was changed after I was born due to birth certificate issues. As you can see, to me it was so im-portant that my son carry my last name. After all, from my gran-dad I am the only grandson to carry his name as my dad was his only son. It was important for me to pass it along to my son. We agreed to name him Trey; I got that name from watching the movie *Boyz n the Hood* in my younger days (as stated earlier). I always liked that name since I was a little boy. I watched that movie way before I was supposed to but always loved the name as that was one of the main characters in that movie.

Tracy and I got married. She had always wanted a big wedding growing up, her grandad giving her away and family and friends there. I couldn't see the value in this and only thought about and worried about the money it would cost, not the celebration of becoming one family and both sides of my family and hers celebrating as we should have. I really did struggle with this; I didn't know the difference and there is no excuse. We agreed to go the justice of the peace. I remember going to get married and, truth be told, we didn't even have a witness there, the lady in the courthouse that worked there was our witness. Tracy wasn't good at explaining her feelings and I wasn't good enough at listening to what she had to say when she had to say it. So here we were, baby on the way, recently married, no money, but living our life thinking that we were doing the right thing. I have learned when two people get married, the only way for it to work the way it is supposed to is to have God wrapped all through each person and the marriage itself. He must be the focus of the marriage and clearly this wasn't the case for us. At the time getting married was something more to lock in our relationship and child on the way than it was an actual promise to love each other for a lifetime. Looking back on it, it was sad, but I am just being honest about what it was and my views of it. In life we do not know what we do not know.

As I stated before, we couldn't see that it wouldn't be long until we had some more issues in our relationship. With the core values not there and the emotions of being pregnant and me wanting to continue partying, guess what ... here we were— another huge fight. This one was one of the biggest we had so far. We went back and forth arguing and yelling and I am the type that I am not going to let something like this go on for too long before I just would leave. We agreed to do just that, I took her to the train station and dropped her off so she could go back home and live with her family. Yes, I did that, I dropped my pregnant wife at the train station to go back home. I couldn't stand the sight of her at this time and she couldn't stand the sight of me either. We agreed, as Tracy would try to get physical with throwing things every now and then as she couldn't express her feelings while being upset without her frustration level going through the roof. I can see that now but couldn't see it then. So instead of me losing it and something bad happening, as I have seen before in other situations, I sent her home; here she was on her way home with no money, pregnant and supposed to call her family to come pick her up when she got there.

Well, God has a way of delivering a message to us even in the heat of the moment. Don't get me wrong; I loved my son, I cared for him, but I had a hard time dealing with her when she got out of control. The train didn't stop where it was supposed to, and then I had to call Tracy's grandparents' house who I had a large amount of respect for and ask them if she was there. Her poor grandmother was so worried. As she was asking me what was going on and I didn't want to get too much into detail, I had to explain she was on a train coming home but I didn't know exactly where she was. Later, we found out the train had gone way past the stop and dropped Tracy and another lady an hour away or something like that past where they were supposed to be. The staff at the train station put them in a cab to come back to their original destination. Now, this was a big lesson for me. Although Tracy was out of control now, and that was on her, regardless of her actions we both had not been responsible with our child in her stomach. Talking to her grandmother was one of the toughest things I had to do in this situation. She didn't have to say anything, I just could hear the worry and disappointment in her voice. Tracy eventually did make it to her grandparents' house in the middle of the night after many phone calls checking in.

I was always the type of person who if you didn't want to be with me or work it out, then my commitment is only as much as the person is committed to me. I am either all in or all out. No in between, for me it is a decision. I did what I thought was right and went out and partied and had a great time doing so. I ended up hooking up with an old friend and we hung out from time to time in a short period of a couple of weeks. I had known her for five or six years. We ended up hanging out way too much past the point of any married man and married woman should.

I felt sorry for what had happened and particularly for Tracy. I would put myself in her shoes and think about how it must feel being back there where she started and how much she didn't like it. I missed her deeply once again. She ended up coming back home with me. So we were back together but didn't resolve anything other than location. I did come clean with her about me hanging out and partying while she was gone. I wasn't proud of it, but I couldn't live without coming clean and being honest. She was hurt and never understood why; my goal was not to get her to understand, it was to get it off my chest so I could live with myself. God's word says everything done in the dark will come to light and to confess your sins, which was something I learned later.

13

THE DIVORCE, BIRTH AND MOVE

Somewhere around this time in my life, my parents ran into some really bad times within their relationship. I do mean bad. They separated and my dad moved back to northern VA and was staying with my grandma. Grandma didn't always take care of herself as much as she took care of others. I sure do love and miss her. My dad ran into some rough times that I had to see him go through. Twenty-five years ... and divorced at the end. It was hard for me to understand and to see my dad go through it. He would call me really upset at times. It was tough and hard for me to watch him go through it. All I could do from time to time was listen. He had talked about how his life couldn't go on without my mom being his wife in it. I was torn at this point because on one end I had seen my mom put up with my dad's actions for many years and on the other I felt a little bitterness toward her because she could fix it at any point. What I didn't see is a lack of understanding what it takes to make a marriage work from my point of view. My mom had already decided to move on with another man and this is what was the toughest to understand from her point of view. In life sometimes people get to a point where they are just ready for change no matter what that change is. My mom had reached that point and beyond. It is strange when my dad was out running the streets and doing what he was doing for all those years of us growing up, my mom had just put up with it. Then the tables turned, and my dad started to care for her deeply, and she started to let go. Wow, talk about change… This happens sometimes in life with good people and relationships.

My dad was hurting in a bad way. The man who never let anything bother him or worry him had come to his knees because of the woman he hurt for many years. My mom wasn't out to hurt him by any means. She was sick and tired of being sick and tired. This was a big lesson in life for everyone to see that we get out what we put in. In life we reap what we sow. None of us could believe it, nor did I want to. I had some conversations with my mom and my dad and who was I to be the selfish one in this situation and not see where my mom coming from? My dad was a straight-up player and disrespectful to her for many years and didn't care back then. He didn't know what he didn't know, right? He watched his mom and dad go through it and not know what love was, so he did what most do, which is carry on and let life cycle, this is a common mistake that many of us make as people. We pass the very pain that we have received, and it never ends. I couldn't imagine life after being married 25 years and raising a family to being alone at that moment. That would have to be a rough place to be in. If I wasn't careful this could easily be me in the years to come.

We were getting closer to Trey being born and we decided it would be a good idea to apply for jobs at State Farm Insurance in Charlottesville and live back in Fluvanna. I did enjoy working at the cable company, but I couldn't see myself doing this and being happy for a long time and I had dreams and goals that I wanted to accomplish, and this wasn't the place to do it. Also, moving to Fluvanna we could live with my mom and be close to her. There is something about my mom that calms down my soul when I am unsure of what to do. She doesn't give me the answers but always listens and is a great friend. With Trey coming I couldn't think of any other person I would want to be close to on this earth; after all, she raised five of us.

We moved to Fluvanna, we all lived together in one big house, my mom had a boyfriend and he lived with us also. We just split the rent in half on the house we were living in. Her boyfriend was a good guy, but it felt strange at first seeing any other man around my mom except my dad. I wasn't going to be the spoiled brat to make things weird between us all. He really looked out for me when he could. We became close over the years.

I had a brand-new car that I had purchased right around the time we got pregnant with Trey. It was a dream of mine to always buy a brand-new car and, truth be told, it was a bit of a headache in the beginning, it had electrical problems and I had to keep running back and forth to the dealer. This was a lesson, a dream to own a brand-new car and it is more of a headache than a used car. They eventually worked the problems out. Trey was going to be born soon and I had a car payment over $400 per month and Tracy and I both made around $22,000 per year. My car payment was what Trey's monthly daycare was going to cost. I did what any other man handling his business would do. I allowed my car to get repossessed. This was only the beginning of a lesson to not live outside of my means. I remember I had another car that my parents had gotten me when I was 17 years old and the transmission was bad in it. While living out in the country and having no car, I decided I would go to the junk yard and buy a transmission and attempt to replace the bad one. It was cold outside as it was wintertime and I had very limited tools and equipment; however, working on this car and it being my only option for transportation I figured out how to put a transmission in a car for the first time ever. I had worked on cars before but nothing as steep as replacing a transmission. It is amazing when something must be done how we can put our minds to it to get it done. A question we should often ask ourselves is not whether we can do something but how necessary it is as all things are possible when we believe.

Tracy and I worked at State Farm in Charlottesville for some time, we worked in two different departments. It didn't seem as though we worked for the same company because the building was so big. We did ride to work together, which was nice. While working there Trey was born. My very first child and my son on top of that. What a blessing... This was one of the biggest blessings I had ever received in my life. I thought I had an idea of what fatherhood would be like; however, I had no idea like most dads.

October 27th, 2001 changed my life forever. What a beautiful bundle of joy. Having Trey was more than I ever imagined. I remember he would lie on my chest and we would sleep a lot. It was an amazing feeling. Everyone was so happy that Trey was born. Here I was, the baby boy of the family having my very own baby boy. I promised myself not only to be the best father that I could be but a better father than I had ever seen or witnessed. You see it is easy for us as humans to criticize our own parents or someone else for what they do not do but harder for us to put it into action. I have always wanted to be the example; I had a vision how life could be if we all treated each other like we should. Little did I know this would be easier said than done and the journey I was on would be a tough one. Sometimes it would seem impossible when looking too far into the future, but taking it day by day makes it seem much more achievable and realistic.

We stayed in Fluvanna for some time and continued working for State Farm, I worked in a department with 29 women and I was the only male in this department. There were some tough days with everyone getting along as they didn't always like each other but liked to hang in small groups. There we made a few friends that we would remain friends with throughout life. Eventually I ended up having a supervisor named Brian. He was a nice supervisor and he and I would talk more on a business front than anything.

There was a position that came open back in northern VA. This was a different position; it was an estimator position. Estimators are the ones that determine what exactly should be done to repair a vehicle on paper for cost and documentation. I applied and got the interview, which was very exciting. After a few months I received word that I got the position. This was a big step for me and the family and I was so excited, but this meant we would have to move again. For me moving around didn't bother me much as I did it so much growing up, it was just another thing for me to do; however, Tracy, being my wife, never liked the moving around. She seemed to like this one though and she really loves city life. Growing up in a small town like Waynesboro I guess this makes sense. It never really mattered to me where I lived. We moved back up to northern VA and stayed with Daniel and his girlfriend. The great thing about Daniel and my friendship is it didn't matter what we had going on, if I had something and he needed it, then it was his and if he had something I needed, it was mine. He allowed us to rent a room in their apartment. We were so grateful and being back in northern VA it was good being back home where I was comfortable and knew everyone. Daniel had been living with his girlfriend for a while. She was nice and just like family too. She was crazy about my boy Daniel and would do anything for my man, anytime, anywhere. So we would party and have a good time. There came a time when it kicked in that I couldn't have all the partying around my son and it was time for Tracy and me to have our own place again, so we decided to move and get an apartment of our own in Centreville, a few miles from where we were currently staying with Daniel and his girlfriend.

Tracy wanted the twins to come and live with us and as I grew into fatherhood, I started to feel bad about them not living with us. After we moved, we decided to bring the twins up to live with us. This didn't last long and the reason it didn't was because of the cost of childcare alone. It was so hard to live off the little money we were making and pay over $200 per week in childcare. Little did I know I was looking at this all wrong, leaving the twins in Waynesboro was one of the biggest mistakes I have made in my life, but it also seemed in a weird way they were where they should have been. We didn't keep the twins up there with us for long at all. They always seemed so safe and comfortable at Tracy's grandparents' house with Judy. They were safe there as Judy also lived there to take care of her parents. As the story continues you will see Tracy and I went through some really tough times and they were better off not having to deal with that directly. Tracy had that short fuse I mentioned and normally I can deal with whatever, but every now and then things got extremely out of control as you have read. The strange thing is that no matter what we would go through, life always felt that we were supposed to be together as in a deeper connection, more than the circumstances we would go through at different times.

As the years went on it was as if God wanted us to be together for whatever reasons there may have been that we couldn't see in those moments or the bigger picture of life period. You see throughout these years I didn't go to church and I really should have, but even though I didn't go to church I always felt connected to God as my grandma planted that seed for me very early in life.

We continued to live in Centreville. While living here we had another big fight. Whenever Tracy and I would get into a huge fight filters would come off and respect would disappear, which is very dangerous in any relationship. Once words are said there is no taking them back and, again, as much as I had a filter, I could only take so much. The Bible tells us to be slow to anger and quick to listen. We had a huge fight and, as much as my temper would flare and I would want to flip out, I always knew I couldn't because people would get hurt and I would get into big trouble.

One fight we had I actually called the cops to come out to play it safe and to cool off and also to get back in the house as whenever things would get this bad, we couldn't be in the same space or nowhere near each other. When the cops showed up, I was sitting outside just chilling out and the very first question the police asked me was, "Did you hit her?" I still remember it to this day. Before they even walked in the house or asked any other questions. I thought to myself, *This is horrible. In most fights this is what most men do in the eyes of the law.* I explained I was the one that called so nothing else happened. We moved past this situation. Just like other times nothing was fixed; in these situations we decided to move on but couldn't until the core of our relationship was fixed—sound familiar?

This is around the time that I met Wayne Stewart. Wayne also worked at State Farm. He was a little older than I was and was he smooth. He walked with grace and I could tell there was something about him that was different from many others that I knew. I couldn't put my finger on it for some time. We would hang out and play pool and listen to music. Wayne was from New Jersey. He would tell me how I had wisdom and I was so patient as I shared stories about Tracy and me with him. Although he would tell me that, I always felt like I didn't have enough patience and understanding, and it was like I was missing something personally. One day, I figured it out as he would share stories from the Bible with me and wisdom and quote the Bible. I wanted to be able to quote the Bible like he could. Naturally, by being himself, he made me want to be better as a man. I had read some of the Bible before but never studied it in depth and given my past issues with reading and having a learning disability, I did not think I would ever be able to quote it like he could. He showed me grace and would share his thoughts and how it related to God's word. He wasn't a preacher or anything but a guy who could tell you exactly what the word says and wasn't ashamed of it no matter where we were. He didn't preach it, but he knew how to apply it to life even in a bar while playing pool. We would hang out every now and then, but when we did, it was like we didn't skip a beat in life. There were times when we didn't hang out for six months at a time, but there wasn't any love loss.

One day, Wayne asked me a question, he said, "Eric, how is Tracy's relationship with her father?" I didn't think much of it. He would ask that question sometimes, but not frequently as if he knew I didn't answer it from the last time. Wayne had a great way of making me think and sharing the truth. The Bible tells us to share the truth; however, we are to share it in love, which means we cannot do it for our own gain because love isn't boastful or selfish.

Finally, one day, he asked me again, and I answered. I said, "She doesn't have one to my knowledge."

He said, "Do you know her father?" You all read earlier in the book that Paul (Tracy's grandad) was the one who raised her. I had met Tracy's father (who he is to my knowledge) one time in a store. That was the only time I had ever had a conversation with the man and that was the only knowledge I had of him at this time for myself.

I asked Wayne, "Why?"

He went on about how important it is for daughters to have a good relationship with their father. He went on to speak on how a lot of times (not all) women will set the standard for men in their life based on their relationship with their dads. This was an example of the wisdom that Wayne carried. Until this moment in my life I had never thought about this or heard about this, but looking around me in this world from my view this connected in many ways on so many levels. It is not saying a relationship between dads and daughters fixes everything; however, looking back to my life earlier and seeing how a lot of females liked that bad boy version of men could be something that was picked up off of TV and not in a real relationship or from the home. This was something I would need to think about over the years and most of all Tracy's view of the men in her life. Could this be connected to some of our struggles in our relationship? I knew about her relationship with Paul, but what about the other men in her life? I share this to share the importance of us men being just that—the father God made us to be—and how that could affect not only our daughters in this moment but the future and generations to come. I remember many times Tracy and I would argue, and she would say, "You are just like all the other men in my life." I never really caught what that meant or the depth of the pain she was carrying.

Wayne and I continued to speak of the importance of life and the relationships between dads and their children. I didn't know him long before this moment, yet he was pouring lessons into me that no one had ever taken the time to explain. He didn't have children of his own back then, but he sure had a lot of wisdom and knowledge. Wayne was planting seeds and helping me think for myself and not just listening or giving me the answers he thought were right. Remember we must share the truth and it cannot be for our own gain but in love. I had no idea about those seeds, but I listened and even took notes from him. Until this point no one had helped me see things differently than via the lens I was looking through in my life and for my relationship. Wayne and I continued being friends and his encouragement to help me think for myself was more than he will ever know. It is one thing to feed a man a fish but a blessing to help a man to be able to fish for himself. One is solving his problem for this moment; the other teaches him lessons that he can live with and pass on forever.

14

THE SEPARATION, PRIORITIES AND WHAT IS IMPORTANT

Tracy decided to get a place in South Riding not far from where we lived together, this is where things got crazier. I was around 24 years old. Things got crazier because I started to second-guess what I really wanted and how we had been fighting for something all these years that didn't seem like it was going to come true. I started to ask myself, *Is this worth it? What about me?* You see when you have two people who aren't focused on each other's benefit, things get messy and, truth be told, when kids are involved, they are the ones who suffer in the long run. So as much as I tried to hang on or thought at least I wanted to, the unfortunate happened. I finally realized I was fighting for something, but I felt like I was the only one. Tracy and I were out of town and got into another fight and it was one of those fights that hurt to the core. Sometimes things would be said in the heat of the moment and in anger and not in love, and I would always feel bad later and apologize. I felt much later in life it was more me coaching her to apologize. This is not the way it works. If you must coach someone into apologizing then it isn't from the heart and no lesson learned, it means history is going to repeat itself. When we got into this fight, Tracy wanted me out of the house. I agreed, but she wanted me out right that moment. I had nowhere to go at the time. Her mom ended up asking her to allow me time to find a place.

The time came when we decided to go our separate ways and it appeared to be for good this time. It was a tough time in my life and our relationship. I realized I loved this woman to the core and I wasn't getting what I needed in return and, clearly, I wasn't giving her what she wanted either. I did what any young man would do. I moved out. I ended up renting a basement of a townhouse. There was something I realized at this time in my life, I realized as an adult I had never spent time on me, never spent time alone. I don't just mean physically alone but spiritually as me in the world. I had moved right from my parents' house into a home with Tracy and became a family man. I never felt like I needed any of the street life in order to live my life. Being with someone is a choice, I was always the type that if you want to be with me cool, but if you don't okay, I have no problem rolling on. This time around was different. I felt like Tracy was made for me and I was made for her, but I couldn't let her take advantage of that. I believe Tracy felt the same way sometimes and that is why she would often not care about how I was feeling.

At this tough time in my life I never, ever wanted my son to call another man "Dad" or to look up to another man how he should look up to me. I had visions of Trey going to another man for advice or someone steering him in the wrong direction in life. Or that someone would harm him in some way, and the outcome would be something I could never live with. My dad had a tough past and a rocky time with my mom, but he was always there physically so this made it important to me. This was so important to me.

I decided to start hanging out as I couldn't stay in the basement all the time. Being in that small room in the basement to me was an embarrassment; there was just enough room for a TV, dresser and bed. I even had my own entrance to the back door through the back gate. It was tough at first being alone, but it wouldn't take long to get my vision right for possibilities. I started going out and partying, making runs to Charlottesville where my family was. Shawn, Lydia and me would go clubbing at night on the weekends. Although it felt like it was fun, I knew in the back of my mind and heart there wasn't any future there. When people are lost in life, trying to put plugs in their life that do not belong there, I can feel something missing, sometimes it's by the look in their eyes or the way they walk or their energy. It may sound strange, but I was feeling like I was lost and missing something but putting in many substitutes that wouldn't last in my life.

Around this time, I started hanging out with Kia. Kia was a friend who worked in Charlottesville at State Farm. She was one of those girls that seemed way out of my league. Some would say she had an eye for me way back when working there, but I can honestly say there was never a pass on either of our ends the entire time while working at State Farm. She was always on top of her game, what I mean by that is she always dressed to the T, always having her hair and nails done, and there is no question that when Kia walked through the departments there were many guys who would just stop what they were doing and flirt with her and try to get with her outside of work. I saw this time and time again. I always admired the way she looked and carried herself but had no interest in sleeping around on my wife or creating major chaos in my life. I felt like I had passed that stage of running around chasing girls. Don't get me wrong; I noticed her and many others. I was an easygoing guy and could live a very happy and chill life, but there was always something that kept me deeply rooted with Tracy. When I moved to Fairfax to become an estimator, Kia and I started chatting via email; yes, this was while Tracy and I were together, but through the many problems I never made advances on Kia nor did she to me. I really thought she was way out of my league and with all the guys that she had in her life and had interest in her why would she ever want to talk to me? She would always ask me questions about guys and share pics of her with her boyfriends. Her boyfriends seemed in shape as in fit and skinny, I was clearly not that. I was always honest and straight up about me being married and I didn't tell her too much about the problems Tracy and I had, but I guess anyone who knew anything about life could sense it as it was that bad.

Kia had moved to northern VA to become an estimator as well from Charlottesville just as I did. There were never any lines crossed on the messages we shared. I considered her a friend and I could tell she considered me one too. Picture this: two people who have known each other for a while as friends end up working in the same location, the same area, same position in the company and then here I am separated from my wife. No brainer, right? We started hanging out together. Tracy couldn't stand the thought or sight of her one bit as she swore she had been chasing me from day one and, as much as that sounded great to me, this was clearly not the case. Kia showed no interest in me at all until this time. Right or wrong, my thought process was if you don't want me then don't care about who I am around or hanging with. I never was about big crowds; I was always low key as in me hanging with a few people but not big crowds. I would get my boy Trey every other weekend and when I didn't have him, I was partying, having a good ole time. At least I thought I was. I would get hung up on the fact that Trey was in the world without his dad daily. When he had nightmares, who was there? When he had questions, who would be there? When he needed life lessons and explanations, who would be there? I have seen some very special dads out there that would take care of their kids and do a great job living in a different home than their children, but I couldn't picture long-term my life being this way or his for that matter. Even though I didn't feel Tracy was treating me correctly I still felt bad for her and Trey and the way our relationship had turned out after all these years. It was as though she was lost and needed me and had no idea that she did. Could it be we both were lost and needed each other?

As time went on Kia and I got closer, it was like hanging with one of my friends, which Tracy and I never took time to do. She was the type that would be down for me, down for whatever whenever. Kia is what we would call back in the day a "Ride or Die" girl. Finally, after all these years of fussing and fighting with Tracy, I finally found the one that would support me in whatever I wanted to do. It's not that Tracy didn't do this; however, we didn't always share the same interests. Sometimes

Tracy would support me, but it didn't feel genuine. It felt like it was only supported because she wanted to do her own thing. This was such a great feeling that I hadn't felt as an adult, as a man, as an individual. Keep in mind Tracy and I had been together since I was 19 years old. I feel as though I didn't know what I wanted in life until I was close to 30 years old. I have always had a cool, laid-back personality and felt like whomever I linked up with I would link up with for life. I wasn't all about creating relationships and leaving women or kids behind in my life. I see many do that and that is something that I never wanted to do, even if at times it was at my own expense. Kia and I would hang out and play pool, she had her own place and sometimes we would just chill there. She gave me a key to her place and everything, which meant she trusted me with everything she worked hard for. For a moment in life I finally felt like I had everything I envisioned my life could be and should be. Kia took pride in being with me. Being proud and happy with someone isn't something you say, it is something you feel, and Tracy and I were missing that, but then something started to hit me on a regular basis. I started thinking about Trey, what about my boy? What about Tracy? What about the twins? I was so focused on not having additional kids and I started worrying, *What if I have a child with Kia (by accident) and then I will have Trey out in the world and I have started something additional that I couldn't finish with him?*

There is a saying, "A night full of passion can cause you a lifetime of pain." This was a scary factor for me. Watching guys have multiple kids and not take care of them scared me and it worried me that I would fall into the same category. Life cycles can get very ugly and continue from generation to generation. I never was concerned about not mentally being there for my kids but financially and spiritually. With me growing up with not a lot (financial availability) it scared me that I couldn't financially or spiritually be there for my boy. I never had Kia around Trey; Tracy would have flipped out in a major way. I had many concerns about how Trey felt. Yes, he was only three, but this was my only seed in the world. My thoughts always were if I couldn't take care of him, how could I ever have another child? Tracy was out doing the very same that I was, partying when she didn't have Trey, and she ended up linking up with a pro NFL player. I didn't know this guy (I know his name and I don't care to share). I always was concerned, you see, Tracy coming from the small town at this time it only makes sense, for me I have never been star struck and pray I never am. I was concerned about how she was being treated—yes, it is stereotypical; however, my thoughts were, *This guy only treats women out in the street like dirt that he is not committed to.* Tracy had a good heart. And, as mentioned, I have always felt that God made Tracy for me and me for her, but Tracy and I would have to get out of our own way in order to let God work. The Bible says a man who finds a wife finds a good thing. I was far from perfect in any way or even doing the right thing, but I would think about her and Trey all the time. It is as if I needed to sacrifice my life in order to break these nasty cycles. My dad was all about himself for many years and I couldn't bring myself to think about me only.

I often wondered what life would have been like if my dad was there more often, if he wasn't out and about doing whatever it was that he was, and my mom, how her life would have been better. I watched her for many years hold down her home and family not worrying about what else was going on outside. I thought about how we as men love our mothers to the core but struggle with the mothers of our children. My mom was the perfect example of someone who showed grace to everyone and anyone who did her wrong. If I could be half the kind person she was I would be an amazing person.

Tracy and I never ran into each other while we were out and about, which was strange but definitely a great thing. We were hanging in the same areas but with different people. I often wondered what it would be like if we did run into each other while out with other people. I imagined it would end very badly. I am not the type of person who hates people. I do know I bury stuff and my thoughts are always turning. I had visions, maybe even dreams or nightmares, of what that moment would be like and I could only imagine that, with Tracy's attitude and him being a football player and my anger for everything that I had put up, with it would turn into rage and we all know what happens when all that mixes. It ends up being a bad situation. It's amazing how in life how some people like me can be cool and calm but walking around holding a bomb of feelings inside due to situations and circumstances. If this is where you are in life in your feelings, it is important to speak with someone and work through those feelings as they can be very dangerous. Now, I don't say that for others to worry about me, it was more of a very sensitive subject, I wouldn't be able to take the fact of seeing Tracy with someone else. I know I couldn't. Thank God it never happened for both of us. Knowing the way Tracy was it wouldn't be good the other way either. It was like we didn't want each other but she didn't want to see me with anyone else either.

There was one day I decided to go pick Trey up from Tracy's place. I got to the door and she answered only for me to find that their electricity was turned off in the house due to not having the funds to pay the bill. Now, growing up for me this isn't anything too crazy, this would happen to people all the time. So, as I am there picking up my son to take him for the weekend,

Tracy was going to stay there as Trey and I were leaving, but I couldn't leave her there in a house with no electricity. It was times like this that it felt like Tracy and I should be together. How could I be off doing my thing, living life and having "My Family" living like this? Even though Tracy and I weren't together she was still my family as she had my one and only son biologically in this world. Tracy would always have that respect and love. I honestly think there are times in life when she would take advantage of this; however, it isn't my place to judge.

As Tracy and Trey came to my little basement room and stayed all the emotions and love came back to me. It was clear to me the only way I could look out for them together was to be together. I ended up speaking to Kia about my decision. As much as she didn't like it, she respected it. That is the type of person she was. Did it hurt? Yeah. Was it tough? Yeah. Could I see myself spending time with her? Yes, but I am an all or nothing kind of guy. I can't focus on my marriage and focus on outside relationships at the same time. I decided I would let go of what Kia and I had. That was a tough decision but one that had to be made as there is no comparison when it comes to my family and son and focusing on these generational actions and curses that I realize I have been fighting for a long time.

It was around this time that I could tell something was bothering Tracy. I couldn't put my finger on it. This was something that seemed to be deeper within her. She would mention her dad from time to time and she had never talked about him before. As I mentioned, I didn't know him outside of meeting him in a store once in the past. I could tell she was seeking answers to questions she had either never asked or never got answers to. The Bible says do not judge and we will not be judged. I would never pass judgment on another man as a father, especially after everything I had witnessed and struggled with myself. This wasn't something that she could get past without the answers she was seeking, and I couldn't help her with what was bothering her, and I had a feeling it had to do with the man she knew as her biological father. She had shared with me that they didn't have a connection or a relationship with any kind of depth on a regular basis, that he only came around her sometimes and not all the time. They had spent time together but not frequently and it bothered her how she could be pushed to the side and only be allowed to see him when it appeared to be convenient. She decided to sit down and write a letter about how she felt and express her concerns about the past and present with questions that she shared with me that she had for him. After she completed this letter, she decided she would mail it to him directly in seeking those answers she felt she needed. She confirmed he received it via mail. I was proud of her for doing so, even though I didn't understand everything she was going through at this time or in her life growing up. This was a time when she needed support and not for me to try to fix it. That is what I did, I supported her.

A few months after she took the time to express her feelings and send this letter, he unfortunately passed away and so he never responded. Tracy wanted to attend his funeral, so we did just that. This was a very tough time for not only Tracy but for me as well. I had thought very little about this until now. I didn't realize until later how someone could have a hard heart in the house of the Lord. The Bible tells us, "Harden not your heart when you hear my voice." Here I was with Trey and Tracy in church at this funeral. The family that I had never met was there and not one person acknowledged her in this service as his daughter, she was not mentioned in the obituary, and I thought to myself, *All of these people got up and spoke about how he was a great man and touched them in so many ways and here I am with the person who is supposed to be his family picking up the broken pieces, paying the price for a debt that wasn't mine to pay and what do I tell my son, his grandchild, the day he asks about him?* This crushed me mentally; however, until this very moment of sharing I have never shared any of my thoughts, my emotions or feelings on this situation to anyone. All I could think of was Tracy and my boys at that moment, all three of them. How did they feel?

To all the men reading this, we must do better; we cannot allow our women and children to pay the price for our lack of commitment, for our lack of understanding of our role and our impact on the lives we are responsible for. I share this to share a vision of my relationship with my grandads as you all have read. Now what about Trey's relationship with his grandads? Does this cycle continue out of control? Someone must stand up and say no more regardless of the price to be paid, regardless of what needs to be done. I say it stops right here and right now with making sure that I renew my mind with a new way of thinking. I honestly do not know the history of their relationship or anything that happened prior to me coming into Tracy's life. What I do know is, no matter the truth or how much it may hurt, people deserve the truth. I say this not in judgment, but I say this because lives are affected on many levels and could be affected in generations to come. We have to think about those that can be, will be or may be affected by our actions in our lifetime.

Tracy and I ended up moving back in with each other and getting another apartment in Centerville, which wasn't too far from where we used to live. There were many lessons in life that I had to learn as life continued as I will continue to share. Things were okay throughout this time. I remember while we lived in this place Trey had his first bicycle and he learned to ride it without training wheels, which was a big deal for me and him.

These were the moments that were on my heart that I didn't want to miss out on, things were going in the right direction and we were enjoying our life again. I was so proud of my boy as he was growing up. It wasn't long after this Tracy and I started thinking of buying a home together. Now, mind you, we never really fixed anything we just kind of agreed to get back together and make the best of it. I later learned how a home cannot stand on a divided foundation, as God's word says.

15

Just Because You Can Doesn't Mean You Should, We Loved That House

Things were going well at my job and my income continued to increase; Tracy also continued to work for the attorney and things were heading in the right direction financially and the future was looking very bright. We both had brand-new cars and were paying big car payments every month, which wasn't a big deal as together we were bringing in over six figures yearly. Think about that—a little boy from the hood coming from where I did and now has a combined income over six figures. Money isn't everything as we will soon learn. As the Lord gives, He can take away. We decided to start looking for homes. Home ownership for me growing up didn't seem that important. I had known very few people who owned a home from a personal level. My grandparents owned their home, but there weren't many, so I didn't understand or care about the importance of it. A lot of us are not educated or taught on how to invest in certain things and how spending money on cars that will get old will only cause us to lose money over time; however, property appreciates over time for the most part. I had heard this in a few movies but never thought about it as a life lesson in person. I was okay with what we had, and we had moved so much I figured why not and having a garage, being the car guy I was, was a good thing.

We looked at a few homes and some of them were nice. We ended up looking at one home that was a foreclosure in Gainesville. The moment we walked in this house it was like, *WOW, I can't believe I could own something like this.* We were living in an apartment somewhere around 1100 square feet give or take and this home was more than 3,000 square feet, it was a four-bedroom, three-level finished basement home. Hard wood floors, big open kitchen and a big front porch. We both were wowed, oh and the two-car detached garage was a lovely addition. So naturally we fell in love with this place. It was a dream come true even if we couldn't get this home that we could be allowed to buy something like this. This is life's lesson: just because you can do something, doesn't mean you should. We put an offer on the home, which seemed at the time like a great offer with the housing market in its current state. We figured once we paid on this home for a year or so we would refinance to get our loan rates in line as our credit wasn't great but just okay. Our original offer was too late as someone else had gotten the bid on the home before we did. We were bummed out. As much as I wasn't excited about owning my own home, the excitement of owning what appeared to be three apartments compared to what I was living in was very exciting. Back to the drawing board we went, looking at other homes.

A few weeks or so later, we received a call that the other person's contract fell through for whatever reason and if we would like to proceed with our offer then now would be the time. I felt two different feelings about this, one I was so excited to make an offer because of the thought of someone coming from my background and growing up in apartments a lot in my life could own something like this. Then the other part of me was feeling this was a big commitment, but owning this home would be a step forward in the life that I dreamed of or at least saw others have and it would fit my life quite well. Once I saw the excitement on Tracy's face, I knew I had to do what I had to do for her, for our family. Finally things were heading in the right direction to happiness. We also had dreams of the twins coming to live with us one day and this home would be great for the space that we would need. We put the contract on the house, and everything was going quite well.

The day of closing on the house I actually had the feeling that we shouldn't buy this home. It wasn't due to the house or anything like that. The payment was steep and almost three times what we were paying for rent at the apartment. We did the math and we would have enough money to purchase this home. Imagine this—no money down, turn-key live-in home, all I had to do was sign on the dotted line and take the keys to our new home. That is exactly what we did. You want to talk about exciting? The little boy from the hood is now making money and able to purchase this big home, which was one of the nicest houses with the porch and all on the street it was built on. It was something about the color setup, the shutters and the porch that were just the right fit. We moved into this house and loved every moment of it. How lucky we were as our hard work was finally paying off.

We had an amazing time living in this house; I had the basement all to myself and a two-car garage to tinker with cars and motorcycles if I wanted to. We had cookouts often and family over. We would play cards and listen to music a lot until the late hours of the night into the morning. Our neighbors were really cool and it all just worked. Tracy and I continued to struggle with our relationship, but the house and life kept us busy. I never really could understand why we just couldn't get it right. After all, I was a good person and she was a good person and most of my life I thought that is all two people needed to have a good relationship. Was I wrong, ever so wrong?

We continued to live in the house and everything was all good, we continued with the car payments and the cookouts and all until one day Tracy lost her job. My income didn't change and stayed the same and now she had to take a job that was 50% of the income of what she was making. That difference we lost alone was enough to cover our mortgage payment and, as I stated, it was already expensive. This is where life started to teach me another valuable lesson. We were in a bind as we were spending all our money as we got it between the cars, motorcycles, house, kids, cookouts, life etc. Very little savings were in the bank; I am talking much less than a couple months of mortgage. This is where times got deeply tough. We continued to live in the house although resources were tight. I had to reach out to a friend for a personal loan to help cover the mortgage a month or two. The tricky thing about this was I couldn't see, *Well, if I can't afford it today, how will I afford it tomorrow?* I know he knew this; however, he didn't hesitate to help.

At this point it was really borrowed time. Tracy's truck was repossessed, and it was a tough and embarrassing time. She loved that truck and me as the man could not stop them from coming to get it, I couldn't save my wife's heart from being broken seeing her truck that she had for a few years be taken away. As time got tougher the house was next. We called the bank to see if they would allow a short sale on the house; to our surprise they did allow short sales. This saves your credit as they sell the house at a reduced rate, so we got back with our same realtor that sold us the house and we got an offer to short sale the home that we loved so much. Well, the bank rejected the short sale. This is where it really got tricky because there was no way we could sell the house for what we purchased it for, and we didn't have the resources to cover the remaining balance.

Just before Tracy lost her job, she had thought about having another child, well, a few things came to my mind immediately—first her tubes were tied as our decision after Trey was born; Trey was getting a little older and I wasn't crazy about the idea, especially the season of struggle we were in. After talking about it for a few weeks we proceeded with having the procedure and we decided to have another child. I had my days where "I felt some kind of way" toward Tracy for pushing so much to have another child. One thing I love about her is she is very persistent, but sometimes that can work against me if you know what I mean. A few months after having her tubes reversed Tracy was pregnant and we were having another child.

Tracy went through a lot of tough times during the pregnancy. She was very sick throughout her pregnancy. She ended up having to have an IV during her pregnancy for months considering how sick she was just to keep her hydrated, nurses had to come to our home to help her and change out her IV. Here we were, tough financial times, home getting ready to be foreclosed on, truck repossessed, my family looking at me as provider and we had another child on the way. Talk about tough times and pressure and not being able to see a way out. Not to mention my wife and son absolutely loved this place. For me it was a big deal, but more for my family going through it than for me to have to move. I moved around so much as a child it was second nature to me. Unfortunately, the time came when I couldn't do anything else to save our situation but to pack up and move. There was something missing though; even though we loved this house, my question to self was did we ever really make it a home? What I mean by that is our marriage wasn't complete; as a matter of fact, we struggled with a lot of the same issues for years. We could never put our hands on what was missing nor did we take the time to analyze what could be missing. We ended up moving up the street and renting a place again. Times didn't really get any easier. Financially it was tad easier as my brother Derrick moved in and rented the basement, but we also knew that wasn't a long-term fix. It was only a band aid for a much bigger situation.

16

THE BIRTH OF OUR BABY GIRL TORIE; THE INTRODUCTION TO PVC

On November 8th, 2010 Torie Renee Folks, our bundle of joy, was born. Little did I know this little lady would turn my view of life into something even greater from holding her and I would have an amazing time loving her. Although I had a tough time seeing the benefits to having another child, God sure had a vision and a plan. We stayed there for a while after Torie was born and then ended up moving again multiple times trying to find our spot to settle down in.

The next place we lived in my dad ended up living with us for a little while. He would live with us from time to time; it seemed like he would live with us and then get on his feet and then move again. This go around he was struggling with his health. He has a non-curable type of cancer and this time he had to take chemo treatments. I've seen my dad deal with this in the past but this time it was different, this time it had my attention in major ways. As my dad went through treatment it was as if it was taking a little out of him at a time. It is so tough to watch your parents struggle with anything. It is almost as tough as watching a child struggle. Life is funny like that; the same struggles others must watch us deal with as children we must watch as adults. It is almost as if that is life's cycles for a reason. My dad ended up finishing his treatments and was doing much better and then we all agreed we would move along with life and around this time my life would take another step to being tougher. Cancer is a tough thing to watch, witness and fight through. The struggle was so serious. As tougher times came Tracy and I had to do something we thought we would never have to do again in our lives and that was move to an apartment. Rent in our area was going up and we just didn't seem to be able to afford it. You talk about embarrassing and shameful, as a man I couldn't even keep a stable roof over our heads. This started to get to us and an already stressed relationship and marriage and individual times would test us beyond what we could imagine.

As we moved into this apartment it seemed that we were at our all-time low. The tough thing about these apartments is even though they were remodeled they were low budget. I normally can count my blessings no matter what, but it was becoming tougher because not only do we live in a world that normally measures success on the things that we have, I had become that partially as well. I came from very little and I can normally see the positive in any situation, but like I said, this was getting tougher at this time in my life and current situations. So just to give a visual, here we were in a two-bedroom older apartment. My family wasn't happy in this space or in a good place at all. It was embarrassing for my friends to help us move in. It was embarrassing for anyone to come visit me. I had friends doing great for themselves and had things going for them and I started to think in my mind, *WHY ME?* Little did I know that was a great question for me to ask myself.

Around the time Torie was born we were introduced to Park Valley Church (PVC). Tracy had taken Trey to an event called Trunk or Treat. It is where the church celebrates a setup like a Halloween theme, but it is more family friendly and during the day and late evening. She had gone one year and told me about it, then another year we went together. It was nice, one cool thing about Park Valley Church and the relationship that was waiting on me was my brother had cleaned the building one time in substitute of the cleaning crew and his boss that I had known since a very young boy as our mom worked for him, he is a member there and on the board there as he helped start the church. When we mentioned to Derrick that we had gone there, he told us about cleaning the building and that his boss went there. So here we were in our lives wondering why and there was a message that we weren't receiving and that we were missing, but it wouldn't be too long before we had some answers and direction to our situations and circumstances. Prior to moving into this apartment, we would go to church every now and then, but we started to go on a regular basis, and this is when God started to open my eyes. The frustration of being in the struggle wouldn't last long without me deciding to move to hopefully make it better. You see I grew up under the impression that when things are tough it is okay to move, it is okay to change your setting. It wasn't in a sense of running from anything but changing and hopefully things would change. Well, what I didn't realize is it doesn't matter where you are, if you don't change your habits, if you don't change your thought process you could end up in a different physical place but in the same mental and spiritual place. Think about that for a moment, a different location physically but the same location mentally. This is where life started to open my eyes even wider.

Times stayed tight and I couldn't see any way out or any light at the end of the tunnel and the little light that I did see appeared to possibly be a train that could run me over. No one wants to be stuck in a tunnel with nowhere to go and a train coming through. I started to take inventory on what I had and what I could move to lighten up the load a bit. Sometimes rent was late, we had a hard time making ends meet just to buy simple groceries, and I am talking diapers, lunch money etc. Tracy was at home and was looking for work, but when daycare is 200 plus dollars a week, it makes it very hard to work and benefit to profit from it. I was making decent money for the area, but it wasn't good enough for a family of four to live comfortably. As I started to look around, the only thing I had left of value was my motorcycle.

I had picked up riding motorcycles a few years back when we owned the house. My dad used to ride motorcycles and I had never thought about it. It was almost as if one day I woke up and said I wanted a motorcycle. Were they dangerous? Yes, but there is no feeling like riding a motorcycle, the freedom, the feeling, the sound, it almost feels as if you are flying. We would ride on Sundays a lot and I could change out the wheels and pipes and put lights all over them to make them look so awesome. We could ride for hours and not even think about how long we were gone or the distance we went. Tracy would support my riding of the motorcycles. She would ride on the back of them from time to time depending on whether we had a babysitter for us both to be gone. This was absolutely my getaway from everything. I could be feeling the pressures of the world and get on the bike for five minutes and feel free from all the issues on my mind. My bikes, like my cars, were very loud. It is almost as if the pipes did the screaming for my voice inside. I absolutely loved this bike, I loved it sometimes more than I knew I should have, but that was my getaway, that was my pride in an automotive way, that was what I could claim pride in and people would say, "Man that is an awesome bike." It made me feel good again that is how I grew up and that was the person I was becoming, value in everything but where the value really is. I had to be a man and stand up and swallow my pride and it was time to let go of my bike. It was paid for and my family could benefit off this, so I did what just about any man would do and I sold it. Again, I never looked in the mirror and said to myself, *This is only going to buy you a few months until you must do something else.*

My job was very stable; however, my income was not going up. I was having a tough time getting my team to perform so I could gain bonuses and things of that nature. As much as I am a positive person, I was feeling defeated, I was feeling down, and the very smile I was putting on for others was starting to fade. I could feel it, my frustration levels were going through the roof inside and I didn't know what to do. I leaned on what I know best, if it isn't working and you can't get traction then change it.

I remember sitting outside one day looking into the sky asking God what He wanted from me. Now, you want to talk about the right question. THIS IS THE RIGHT QUESTION to ask!

I didn't get my immediate answers that I was looking for as we know the Lord works in mysterious ways. I got the bright idea of, *You know what, we are going to move back to Waynesboro. It will be awesome to see family all the time, my mother and Tracy's mother live there and it is a great idea. We can get a house for cheap rent and I can make a little bit of money there. A lot less than I am making, but we will be just fine.* Tracy hated the idea, to move back where she left was not acceptable. She did not like to spend more than a couple of days in this place and I was asking her to move back there. With the state our marriage had been in for some time I didn't leave her much option. It was decided and we were moving. I had decided after seven years of working hard for the company I'd had enough of northern Virginia, and I was not coming back. I decided to put in my notice to quit.

This for me was one of the toughest things I had done in a very long time, even after the moving and losing the house, cars, etc. I was going to leave a company that had supported me. It wasn't the company; it was the relationships I had developed. I almost cried when I told Johnny Krauss I was leaving, he was the COO. It hurt me more than I am sure it had hurt him. He'd seen many come and go and the company, just like any other, would be just fine with or without a single person. Johnny was one of the owners, but he had looked out for me for many years, whether it was with words of encouragement, financial help or looking out for my family and booking us time at the company's beach house. He and Jerrod Dalton had been there for me in ways no one ever had, I considered both friends and mentors. This was tough and would seem crazy, not to mention I had to tell my team that absolutely loved me, and I loved them just the same.

Everyone was in shock. Johnny and Jerrod were two of the most humble and giving men that I had met in my life, they were supportive and led by example and both had taken time out for me to help me. Not so much put a band aid on my problems, but to invest in my thought process and do their best to help me see the vision of life, a better vision than I had been looking at or having. These two men right here believed in people and didn't mind helping others. They both welcomed me and my family into their homes to visit and hang out. Both of their wives, Kelli Krauss and Jennifer Dalton, are very special and had accepted my family into their homes for dinner and celebrations and we had met their families as well. It is tough when you come from what appears to be very little and you meet someone who appears to have it all; to think they would accept you, to think they would invite you in and not only invite you in but treat you like family is an amazing blessing. I can pick up the phone today and call either Jennifer or Kelli and they will accept me for who I am and my family as well. They both have purchased gifts for my

children out of the kindness of their hearts. Still to this day I haven't met anyone quite like them with so much grace for others. They helped me with my vision to elevate my thought process. God will put people in our paths who can help us on our journey, and we can help them as well. If you want to get on someone else's level, then you should spend time with them. People will help you to get to their level if that is what you really want and you listen. Elevate your company and elevate your lifestyle.

Johnny and Jerrod have it all (in my eyes) and still would take time to look out for me and mine. That is why this was so difficult for me. I still remember the day I told Johnny I was leaving just like it was yesterday. He asked me why and I told him and, as much as he didn't want to get this news, he respected my decision and my why. He asked if there was anything he could do. Think about that for a second; my life, my problems, but this man is humble enough to ask if he can do anything to help change it after all he had already done for me and my family. I respectfully declined, of course. I felt at this very moment that I was making a mistake; as the words came out of my mouth I wanted to take them back, but I felt like I couldn't stop what was in motion. I had given my word and made my decision and no matter how tough things got I was going to do my very best. That was it, decision made, so my family wasn't happy, my job wasn't happy, my team wasn't happy; those who cared for me and loved me knew it wasn't their choice of what they would like to see, but everyone, I do mean everyone, respected my decision. Somehow, some way this was going to work out for me and the family. I knew it but couldn't see it at that moment.

17

FEELING LIKE A FAILED MAN, I CAN'T TAKE IT ANYMORE SOMETHING HAS TO CHANGE

We had been going to church on a regular basis and I started to look to God for answers and my faith started to build even though life was tough. My relationship wasn't where it should or could have been, but I started to wonder want He wanted from me and how I could get out of my current situation. I would do just about anything in the right form of course to provide for my family. I no longer needed a large house; I no longer needed a new car, I loved these things, but my thoughts on my wants versus needs started to change. I remember sitting outside at the apartment looking up in the sky wondering what God wanted from me. Little did I know He would supply the answers in his timing and not mine. We were liking Park Valley Church, and this is the first time Tracy and I committed to going to church as a family and husband and wife. I didn't fully understand my position as a husband, but I thought I did, and I would soon find out how to lead my family in the manner I was supposed to. In life often we don't miss things until they are gone in truth.

We ended up making the move to Waynesboro. Tracy was really upset about the decision I made. She was so against it and I was on a mission. I needed change so badly after the years of going backwards and falling in a hole that I couldn't dig myself or my family out of. If we were going to work hard and be limited, we were going to have a house to relax in and having my mom and Judy a few blocks away was perfect. I did something that I am not proud of, I told her since we only had one income coming in that we were making this move no matter what. I didn't explain my feelings; I didn't consider hers; I made the call. I do understand sometimes that is needed, but not like this is something I would learn later.

We moved to Waynesboro, I started working at a body shop near where we lived, and things were so slow I found myself being bored. The fast pace that I was tired of and the noise and chatter of life were not there. At first it was nice to breathe for a bit as I felt like I was choking and couldn't breathe in life. It wasn't long after that we started missing church big time. We had fallen in love with Park Valley Church and I didn't realize it.

Moving to a new area and not having the foundation of church and God in our family was not helpful at all and wasn't going to help us grow. Tracy and I had had a rough marriage at times. I always felt as if God put us together to grow together and look out for each other even though we couldn't see it just yet. I know we needed to continue going on even if things didn't seem right from time to time. This also helped me with patience and looking in the mirror to do better and be better.

Within a couple of months of being in Waynesboro I realized living a few blocks over from our mothers wasn't much of a benefit if we didn't go visit them that much. Also, the twins lived there in Waynesboro and they were busy doing their thing and living their life. I went from seeing eight plus customers in an hour to seeing maybe eight customers in a few days. This may sound silly, but I realized that I didn't really make a mistake, but Waynesboro wasn't for us long term. This was clear after just a few months. Tracy told me that she gave me six months prior to us moving there that I would be looking for something else. She wasn't always right, but she wasn't always wrong, and as much as I didn't want to admit it she was right. I would look up to the sky for direction, I would ask God for direction and as silly as this may have seemed His plan was not for us to stay in Waynesboro long term. I started looking for what was going to be next, but I started looking to God for direction in what to do next and

He started to provide options for us. I later learned and now understand God's word says, "Submit the plans you have to me." His word also says, "I know the plans I have for you, to prosper you." I had never thought deeply or prayed on either one of these verses. I had a lot to learn and life was teaching me what and who to focus on and who not to focus on.

Two things had come up, I hooked up with my cousin down in Atlanta and he was setting me up for a future move and although we had only been down there once or twice, it felt awesome—the people, the cost of living and the thought of a new area to live. I was all in, that is for sure. I started to look for work down there in the Atlanta, GA area. Then, out of the blue, a guy from our old company Craftsman Auto Body reached out to me and asked if I wanted to come back. I had learned many years prior in life that the most expensive thing to have is a closed mind and I was open for ideas and opportunities. I listened to what he had to offer, and it wasn't what I had hoped, but it did spark my thought process to the idea of possibly coming back. It hadn't crossed my mind since we left. I also knew I not only had a friend in Johnny and Jerrod and the management team, but I had family I could reach out to and really see what was there for me. There was one question that I had to answer; however, I wasn't thinking about it. You see in life we can often get excited about change, but sometimes we skip the real question of what

will be different. Change isn't always a good different and sometimes we get so excited about change we could very well end up
back in the same position we left.

As time went on, I talked more with my cousin and got
more excited about the move to Atlanta. I had sold my car after
we moved to Waynesboro as I didn't have the money to fix it
and I started to see that it was going to take a miracle to change
the outcome of us staying there and at some point we were going
to end up in a tight situation again. We could stay and coast, but
with business being very slow there and the income being set, we
couldn't save anything to stack any money in the savings. I decided to pursue the Atlanta move and found a company there to
interview with to see if I could get a job in the collision business
down there, which I was already in. I had an interview set up
with them and decided to make the trip. Tracy was not crazy
about the idea at all; however, she was right there with me. I
think she would have done almost anything not to stay in
Waynesboro. She loves her family but does not like to be in the
small-town setting. I went to Atlanta and had my interview and I
got the job. I prayed to God for direction, the break I needed
was the break that I no longer felt I needed as I started to get refreshed and ready to get back in the game. Growing up in northern VA, Atlanta would be a great change and I could so see us
living there. I thought I had it figured out as the plan was for me

to go down ahead of the family and link up with my cousin, you see he has it going on and he is someone I look up to big time, not only in just how successful he is but also the way he carries himself; he is a businessman and his home and love for his wife and the Lord is something that I can feel from him. He wants others around him to succeed. I hadn't known him closely for a long time as he is my mother's first cousin and a little older than me, but I really felt a connection. Naturally, when we look up to others, we often want to know what it would be like to duplicate what they have going on. Not in a jealous way, if he could help me get where he was then life would be great. It made me want a better life for Tracy and I and our family.

Just as the Atlanta move was coming up, I started to talk with Jerrod about going back to northern VA and then one day Johnny called me, and I always felt a connection to him. I always felt that within his control he was always down to help me out and he understood the struggle. It is something about his personality that it is almost as if he walks with grace and understanding. Here I found myself with options to pursue my move down south to a place I really felt excited about or make a move back to where I came from. I was getting excited about possibly going back and one day I was on the phone with Johnny and Steve Welch. Steve was my direct manager for years and this man knows how to run a business. He knows the pieces to the puzzle that are needed to run a successful business. I had learned a lot from him over the years as he had been nice enough to pour into me and help me on my journey to be a manager. Steve has a way of asking questions that make you think. He will not give you the answers directly but will help you seek them for yourself, which is where the important growth happens, and I needed to start thinking differently. I had worked directly with Steve for years and he cared about my thought process and my family. He said, "I would love for you to come back, but you obviously left for many reasons, why come back?" This wasn't a question I was ready to answer, nor had I asked myself. I gave him a quick answer and thought to myself, *That is a great question.* I found myself looking in the sky for answers, I didn't know where to go, but I knew I couldn't stay where I was.

I had already had a start date for the Atlanta move. I was going to stay with my cousin and my family was going to hang back while I went ahead and came back for them at a later time. That was the plan. The problem with that is that Atlanta was eight hours away and a weekend home every couple of weeks just wouldn't cut it. Both of my kids were young, and I was going to leave my wife to take care of the family for weeks at a time by herself and all alone. This only made sense in my mind because of the situation. Sometimes we hear what we want to hear and see what we want to see as a matter of fact. I have always been a "do what you must do in order to get where you want to be" kind of person. I soon found out that a lot of times we only must do what we need to because we didn't do what we were supposed to. As the start date came closer and the conversations around commitments continued, I decided that, even though I had to swallow my pride, I would turn down my offer to move to Atlanta. Johnny and the team had a new center that they wanted to open, and they offered it to me. Even though I quit them and left they were ready to allow grace on my end and give this relationship another try and to allow me not only to come back but to go into a completely different direction. They also were pairing me up with Jon Hart as my mentor and area manager to help me with things as they came up.

Jon used to run our most successful shop and was one of the realist guys I would come to know. I knew of him as he helped me during my last few months of being at my old center prior to moving to Waynesboro, but little did I know he would impact my life and leadership skills way more than I had ever imagined. Tracy and I still struggled with our marriage and things still didn't feel right as husband and wife. We couldn't get it together and it was bothering me. I was always a good guy and tried my best to do what was right. She was a good woman; however, I would find out soon that isn't always good enough to make a marriage work.

18

AT THE LOWEST POINT, HUMBLE YOURSELF, GOD WILL ANSWER THE QUESTIONS YOU ASK IN HIS TIME

Tracy really wanted to go back to northern VA, she loved that area. As we agreed it would be best to go back to northern VA, we decided I would work up there for a while and come home on the weekends. This was going to be a task; however, two hours away in northern VA and home every weekend is much better than every few weeks and being eight hours away in Atlanta. At this time things seemed crazy; here I was moving my family back to the very same area I had just moved from only months later. I thought to myself, *People are going to think I have lost my mind and laugh at me like, "What is this guy doing?"* There was some truth to me losing something; however, it wasn't my mind. I had lost my focus and vision. At least I thought I did lose some of my mind. I continued to lean on God and think about what He wanted for my life. We missed our church and I could see the difference going to church was making in my family and my marriage.

I had to figure out the car thing as I didn't have one. I found an old Ford Taurus that needed a fuel pump replacement. I bought the car a week or two before I was supposed to start traveling 125 miles one way on Sundays and back every Friday. This car had a major break down right before I was supposed to start, and the fix was going to cost way more than I had paid for it and what I had available to spend on it. Now what was I going to do? This was another setback and rough situation. Here I was, no money, a broken car and I need to start working out of the area within a couple of weeks. I posted the Taurus for sale as there was no way I had the money to fix it. I found someone to buy it, believe it or not, as it was; knowing it was broken they bought it from me. Can you believe that? Yes, they did. Now I needed to find a car. I looked at some buy now pay later car dealers and I just didn't feel right getting a car payment. This is where Jerrod and my conversations really started to kick in from the past. Jerrod taught me if you cannot afford it, then do not buy it. Also, he advised me to calculate how many days, months, and years the cost of an item would have you work to pay off. I realized with very little to no money I had made some very bad choices and continued to pay for them—the house, the cars, the bikes. The question of what is going to change, which was asked prior to accepting the job back at Craftsman Auto Body, is what I needed to start asking myself. BOOM! There it was—change.

The Bible says "to worry about nothing, but instead pray about everything." As I was really worried about how this would work, Judy said her neighbors who had bought her 1995 Nissan Sentra was selling it as their mother no longer needed it and would let us have it for 500 dollars. I thought no way that car would last at first, but I was praying and worrying at the same time and here was a solution. I said, "SOLD!" I went and bought the car. This was the very same car my Judy had purchased brand new many years ago and here I was getting ready to drive this car. Do you think this was possible? God works in mysterious ways. Could she have purchased this car back in the day for it to save my job at a later time without knowing it? I was so embarrassed to drive this car. I was a car guy, what was I doing driving this car? I was better than this and didn't think I would ever drive something like this, it was the roughest car I ever owned as far as looks and style. There was a lesson for me to learn through this. I am never too good for anything and God will take us and break us down to nothing to build us up within, reminding us we have always had everything we need and we are measuring our value in the view of the world.

I had fallen to the bottom of the bottom. It wasn't long before this car that I thought I was too good to drive it would teach me many life lessons. One of those lessons is that I am never too good for anything and driving a car that is paid for, no matter how bad it looks, can be one of the best things to do, if it is all you can afford; it will take me from point A to point B. This car and situation humbled me so much. Another lesson was, as this was all I could afford, to appreciate it. One time, I was driving and the car broke down in the morning on the way to work. When it is all you have, you tend to look at it as a blessing and not an embarrassment. This lesson was big as my first thoughts were, *How will I get around? What do I have to get back and forth to work?* And the answer was nothing. I had spent most of my adult life spending every dime and dollar I had on the things and people that I loved but not saving.

Don't get me wrong; I still wished I had those things, but that is great when you can afford it; when you can't, then you can't. It is that simple. Rich folks get rich by saving money, not by spending it. I learned that broke people stay broke by not only spending all they have but also more than they have and that is where debt comes into play. The Bible even speaks on how a fool spends all they have. It is all by choice, yet most of us get caught up in life looking at what others have or by buying what we want. I remember a conversation that Jerrod and I had, he said that he doesn't buy anything that he doesn't have the money in the bank for or he will get zero percent interest rates. I was nowhere near ready mentally or financially to think that way, but he was right; although the Nissan Sentra was rough to drive, I didn't have to make monthly payments on it or pay a bank for borrowing money that I didn't have to pay for a car to drive. These are the lessons we need to teach and many can learn from. When you borrow from your own money, things change and life is so much more balanced. I always thought there was some magic or that was something I could never get to; however, I found out later through God's grace and mercy that it is about my thought process and not just doing things because we can.

Kenny Coleman was a guy I used to work with and he had a nice-sized house with a bedroom in the basement and was going to rent me a room I could stay in during the week and I would come home on the weekend. I still remember the very first day I left to go stay with him. There was a snowstorm coming and it was so hard to leave my family, to kiss my babies and know I wouldn't see them for five days for the very first time in their lives. Broke my heart to pieces. This was very difficult for me. My goal was to leave on Monday mornings and come back Friday nights. I later found it was much easier to leave while they were sleeping and not while they were awake. I remember as I left the first day I cried, frustrated and sad that I had allowed this to come about, but shortly after I prayed to God that He would make this alright and I got into go mode. Not to mention Tracy and what she had to go through taking care of the kids by herself for four or five days at a time. There was times I would go to bed early during the week, not because I was tired, but it was easier that way; the days would go by faster by going to bed early, the days seemed shorter. So I could hurry up and get to Fridays to get home. I would talk with the family every night prior to going to sleep. It was nice for Tracy and me to miss each other. Things seemed okay and the plan was for us to do this for six months and stack up some money.

Kenny and I spent a lot of time together and I realized for him and I that was a time for us to fellowship and get to know each other on a deeper level. I found that he is a good man and has a huge heart for people and life. He shared his story with me over time as we spent time driving to work together and hanging after work. The wild thing was it was almost a portion of my life I had never lived. I moved in with Tracy right after moving from my parents' house and I never felt the need to live alone and live the solo life, but I realized that we all should spend time out on our own. Not to party or anything like that, but getting to know ourselves and to see what life has to offer. We spend so much time getting to know others and fitting in this groove of life that we forget to find out who we are. I definitely wasn't looking to live this lifestyle it just had its moments.

I remember I couldn't wait for Thursday nights as I knew I would be traveling home the next day and I couldn't wait every Friday to get home and spend time with the family. I missed them. It was also nice to come home after being missed sometimes. We continued doing this for some time; the plan was to make this work for six months. We came to realize six months was a very long time to be away from the family and for my family to be alone every week Monday through Friday. It was nice to have so much family around and we could rely on them if anything came up or Tracy needed help while I was gone. So after about two months I knew this wasn't going to last much longer. I was tired of running the road and although Tracy did an awesome job of taking care of the family, it was time for us to plan to make the official move back to northern VA. Tracy was so happy as she loved the area in northern VA versus being in Waynesboro. While in Waynesboro Tracy and her mom's relationship got a lot better and they got closer. The kids loved to see their grandmothers on a regular basis. Both of our mothers understood exactly what we wanted to do. Although they would miss us, they had always been supportive. We didn't have our exact goal of the amount money in the bank we had planned, but I got to the point where I would rather have my family with me side by side and struggle a little than for my family to be apart. I missed having my family, I missed the meals, I missed seeing my kids every day and seeing them to bed at night. They say you don't often miss things until they aren't with you every day. It's the small things that really are the big things in life.

So here we are, I am excited; on a Friday I took off and grabbed the U-Haul on the way. Johnny Krauss and Jon Hart whom I reported directly to for work were always super cool about me taking off a little early on Fridays and looking out for me making sure the family was good. What I mean by this is if I needed a day off, they wouldn't dock my pay and things. I didn't take advantage of the fact. I remember I needed the money so I would grind it out and there was a day after a holiday, I think it was Christmas, and Johnny told me to take off and I had to make sure I wouldn't lose money for that day. His exact words were, "Go spend time with your family." So I was excited to get to Waynesboro with the truck and load it up and bring my family back. At this time there were no thoughts on how silly I felt moving there for a few months and moving back. It was as if I was refreshed like I had needed a break to get my mind right. The family was excited as well. I could feel it. My man Gary "Sleepy" came down to help us move. Sleepy was always there for us not only the many times we moved, and I am sure he was tired of moving our stuff, but he would show up every time. I didn't have a lot of help at all and he came down to help. I can always count on him to help me out. I did my best not to inconvenience him; even when we moved down he came down and drove the truck back to return it. I can always count on him.

Sleepy is one of the first people in my life who was close to my age and taught me about family outside of family as an adult other than Daniel. Don't get me wrong; when I was growing up, I had a lot of people who blessed me with care and wisdom, but as I got older those relationships kind of got quiet outside of my man Daniel and Wayne. Daniel and Sleepy are a lot alike in values of being there. They are the type of brothers that will drop what they are doing and come help. It doesn't matter what they have going on; if they can be there they will. If they must move things around, they will be there. I always felt like they are there for me more than I am there for them. That is the great thing about life. For a lot of people seeing is believing and they show me the example of what I should be, what kind of friend. Life isn't only about when things are convenient for us, it is about helping others. Sleepy is a leader of his family and someone I look up to. Even though we didn't know each other for much of our lives, he taught me a lot in the short time I've known him. He is the type that lives his life. He works for the government, was in the military from St. Louis, had been over to Germany and now he is here. Not only is he a great friend, he has his life together. Financially I learned so much from him. We would do things together. People would ask if we are brothers when out in public in a store or something. We liked a lot of the same things, video games, motorcycles, cars, family, etc.… Sleepy is a straight up handy man around his home as well. He is smart and isn't afraid of anything that I have ever seen. He has college degrees and all, I can tell he thinks differently from others. I have never told him how much I look up to him, but I always have for the very things I explained above.

I met Sleepy back in about 2007–2008; when we had our house in Gainesville, he and his family lives in the neighborhood. Our wives became best friends, Tracy and Kesha, and our kids did the same. Trey was around the age of their oldest and Torie was at the age of their youngest two. We all just get along in great ways. He will tell you like it was, too, not afraid of how you feel, just a keep it real kind of man. Sleepy and Kesha will invite us into their home, and we would go on vacations together as families and enjoy each other's company. Kesha is very nice, and I felt like she never judged me through all the moves that I had to make. She fixes a mean carrot cake, which I love, and would cook good dishes for us all to eat. They always showed us grace no matter what we had going on.

We loaded up this truck and we were on our way back to northern VA to bring the family back. We moved into a nice townhouse in a gated community with the golf course at the back of the houses. This is where God really started to show me some things in my life and change the outcome of my life and future. I came to realize that I had to work harder if I was going to have a different and better outcome than what we had before. Steve's question of what would be different was still on my mind. As good as things were going, we would have to do things differently in order to have a different outcome and when God is blessing your mission, we must give Him something to work with as I always say, but He is an unlimited God, that is for sure, and as we put in good He will multiply our mission. We were getting settled in our new rental place and it was nice to have space and we were right around the corner of our old neighborhood that we owned the home in where Sleepy, Kesha and their family lives along with many other friends and family. Trey got to go back to school with his old friends. Everything was good. With the family being back up in the area together everything seemed on the up and up. Things were going very well with work.

19

In Order to Get Change, You've Got to Change, As All Things Are Possible to Those That Believe

A s I mentioned, we were opening a new center. It opened around 2013 and it was exciting to have a business that I was a part of from the opening. It is one thing to come into a business already running, but this was a brand-new opportunity to make my mark from the opening. This shop was three times the size of my old center and if I was going to be successful, I was going to have to do things differently. Example processes would have to go into place for this center. I remember Johnny Krauss sitting me down and saying, "Eric, I do not need a doer; I need a leader to hold people accountable," as that was my history of management. He said. "If you run around trying to do every-thing, you are going to kill yourself. This building is too big."

And he was right. I couldn't and wouldn't be able to touch everything that happened in the store. I would have to delegate and trust others to do their job and coach them up as they needed too.

I was blessed with roughly 30 people on staff at any time. This was an amazing opportunity and the center was beautiful for a body shop. One of the great things about this opportunity was that I was able to see it transform from what it was into what it became and that alone gave me an appreciation of how clean we should keep this place. When you see something from scratch, it changes things and creates an appreciation for it that is deeper than walking into it. There was a lot of construction and hard work that went into this building, not to mention money, and I was trusted with it. I am talking even down to mopping the floors and understanding the pride that went into the construction team's hard work. I also knew that all eyes would be on me and my team and our ability to take it from opening day and run with it as far as we possibly could. I knew some others doubted my abilities to lead this team in a strong way because of my past reputation and results. People are quick to judge and slow to forgive, but you have people like Johnny and Jerrod that believe, change can happen.

We opened this center and it was an awesome thing to be a part of, it was nice to lead this team and have a new vision for what we were going to do and most of all the possibilities to take it to the top performer in the company. We worked very hard and most of all had fun and it wasn't long before this center was performing in great ways and I had no idea that this opportunity would lead to a future promotion. I didn't focus on what tomorrow was going to bring; we focused on today, which is what we had in front of us each day. The Bible tells us to focus on today as tomorrow will have it's on troubles. It felt great to push it to the limit and for people to come in and like the production that happened in this center. From a business standpoint things were heading in the right direction.

It wasn't long after the center opened that we would find that Craftsman Auto Body was being sold to a new company. As much fun as we were having and grinding out, the change of companies didn't seem like a huge deal. Joining a much larger company meant we would hopefully have room for growth that we wouldn't have in Craftsman due to limitations of positions due to the size of the company. Some prefer larger companies, and some do not. The new company, Caliber Collision, purchased Craftsman and we now were joining a much larger team in 2015. I had mixed feelings about this as Craftsman was my home team and always held a special place in my heart no matter what the past or present proposed. We went from being a part of a 25-center team to over 200 centers with Caliber Collision.

Tracy and I were going to church as we should on Sundays and things were heading in the right direction as far as our life, family and work. Could this be? Could we be on the rebound or what I would call rebuild of where we were? I knew if this was to continue, we would have to do things differently. I started to feel and see things as if we only get one shot at life and if we were going to build this life together or continue living this life together there was only one way to do it and that was the right way—with God at the base of our marriage. I remember sitting in church one day and Pastor Barry mentioned that in a marriage God must be at the base like a foundation of a home or building or anything you are creating or building. We cannot build a good relationship on a foundation that isn't solid, and the only way is with God at the base. At some point our spouses, friends, children, parents will all let us down if we are only focused on each other and not the greatest, which is God. Only He can help us see why we should be together and His word explains why we struggle.

After the acquisition of Craftsman Auto Body by Caliber Collision, which is a company that loved to celebrate all their wins, it was different. There were so many things at Craftsman that we were not exposed to, financial statements as in Profit and Loss statements (P&L'S), a major focus on culture. We had a great culture but didn't fully understand the importance of it.

Culture is one of the greatest things we can focus on to be successful. Caliber came in and taught us how to run a successful business in and out, front to back, and was so transparent about the operations and it made sense. My team continued to work very hard and I started to help other locations with their operations as well. It was tough at first to go into someone else's center and discuss the operations; however, if I was truly going to make it to the next level, I would have to be able to have these discussions. I didn't focus on the next level, again success was focusing on the day to day. I found that most of the time the struggle is in the leadership of the teams and the leader being able to believe in themselves and their ability to lead the team and help the team believe.

I remember one time working at the center and the CEO and COO came to visit. This was the very first time I met them, and they walked in and we greeted each other, introducing ourselves of course. They walked the center with me and looked at what we call the CSEP board (Customer Excellence Program), this is how we measure our customer experience, and they gave me a fist pump for our results. Here were the CEO and COO showing me love in a center and team I was blessed to be a part of building by the grace of God. This is one of those moments that just makes me say WOW even still to this day.

20

GOD'S FAVOR, IT'S ALL A PART OF HIS PLAN

Shortly after helping other centers I was promoted to operations manager, which was very similar to a regional manager position. This was an amazing opportunity. It was around this time I was actually gifted something that couldn't have come from anywhere else except for God I tell you. Someone who was in a great financial position and didn't have to worry about money directly wanted to see my family and I looked out for in the long run and gifted us stocks in a company that was growing rapidly. Only God could send this blessing from heaven. I had never thought about stocks or understood how they worked, it didn't take long for me to do research on the web. Think about that for a moment, I knew nothing about stocks, and someone gave me a large amount of them that one day would be worth quite a bit of cash not just a stock investment.

When you come from where I come from and your retirement is now on another level due to someone else helping you out because they want to bless your family, what a blessing it is from God. I am forever grateful for this person looking out for me. For them to look at me and say, "Eric, I wanted to do something nice for your family. I have seen how much you have been through and this is from us to you as there were a few of us that made the decision to give you the stock." I was shocked and blown away. Again, at this moment, I knew they would make an impact, I really didn't know how much at this time as stock value is as only as good as when you sell it. A guy like me never thought about stocks, never; it wasn't even something that I had heard of on a regular basis. One time, a guy I worked with said his wife had made some investments in stocks, so she no longer had to work due to her investments in the past. That was the only conversation I have ever had regarding stocks and here I was, someone was gifting me something so valuable because they respected the hard work and hustle they'd seen me putting in.

I continued to help with whatever I could at work. I ended up being blessed and over-seeing four centers to start and then another center added. I struggled as an operations manager, but I would never give up and no matter what they put on my plate I would take it on. My thoughts were, *If you want to give me the center that struggles the most, I will give it my all and I will do it with pride and joy. It will be a struggle and I may not be the best, but I will always give it my best.* I learned quickly either you had to outsmart people or outwork them. Either way was a path to success. I would start my days at 5:00 a.m. and work until 7:00 or 8:00 p.m. if needed. You see I was at a disadvantage not being the smartest guy like some others were in my mindset at the time. Caliber invested in us as individuals. We had to go through leadership training and some of this training was so intense. I remember my first major training. This training was so intense for me as a man and individual on this earth. It brought out many struggles from the past. It didn't matter what the past was, either issues with people, parents, life, etc... This training would have you pumped up one moment and crying the next. Intense, but it also helped me to overcome many fears and to look at my ability to break through any barriers I felt that life had put in front of me. Public speaking and expressing my feelings were some of the toughest hurdles in my life.

Even as I write this book, I must give credit to my trainers at Caliber. They are awesome people and a few days training at Caliber has helped me minister people, speak publicly, and write this book. There is nothing that is in your past, present or future that you will not be able to overcome or achieve, you have to believe because God is with you every step of the way and wants you to be successful while giving Him the praise and glory. I often ask myself, *What is next?* A lot of times we get in our own way and we must push through. It takes courage to do the things you have had anxiety, worry and doubt about your entire life. That may seem simple to some, but it is so serious for many. These things can allow us to become paralyzed in a sense and not allow us to move forward at all. Think about that; I have been carrying these stories of not being enough most of my life, but in the back of my mind and in my vision, I would dream of becoming and being that example for others even feeling like the odds were against me. This training helped me understand that we all struggle, sometimes with the very same things, but we continue to believe the stories in our heads of why we cannot do certain things. This is where faith comes in big time. As I write this, the verse "I can do all things through Christ whom strengthens me" comes to my heart. We must live life in such a mindset understanding God's promise is that He will never leave us or forsake us, and we must lean on that promise no matter where we are in this season of life.

Caliber had chosen me of all the 10,000 employees (at the time) to do two Caliber inspirational videos. Can you believe this? You can google today "Caliber Inspirational video" and "Eric Folks" and find the videos. I WAS BLOWN AWAY AND STILL AM TO THIS DAY! This was another area only God could be working in. Picture this, after of all my struggles, all my failures, quitting, but not giving up and realizing I had to get back in the game and a company of this magnitude wanted me and my story to represent them to others joining the company and they would ask me questions like, "Why do you do what you do?"

It was around this time I started to understand about our "Why". You see many go around and through life not understanding or asking themselves why they do what they do daily. Truth be told, when someone asked me for the reason I do things it came naturally, but I never sat down and understood the "why" behind what I do. As they asked and I explained, it all connected with me. My mentor Jon Hart walked every step of this move with me. He was the first person in my life that I had followed and understood that he leads his life with integrity and isn't afraid to say it to anyone. I have known a lot of people who have integrity, but to lead with it every day even when it means in the world's eyes you could or may lose something. The very first question a lot of times with him is around integrity. This could mean losing a job or telling someone to their face you have a problem with them with respect of course. I hadn't seen anyone in my lifetime that I worked with day in and day out that operated this way. It taught me to be a better person and better man and he is all about family first. Regardless what the outcome will be, he taught me so much in actions around his integrity.

Family first and work second. Lots of people say it, but to see someone indeed live life through actions was amazing.

We completed the videos and Steve, who was now our vice president, said some great things about me that I would have never thought he would have said in a million years and it set me on fire. It really connected with me and pumped me up. I can tell you when someone believes in you, it can make all the difference in someone's life. The Bible speaks about how the tongue is powerful and, just as it can cut someone down, it can also build someone up. I had witnessed this directly and most do not realize the very power that they have in their words. I haven't had a self-esteem problem; however, I often stay in my lane and when I know someone is counting on my directly, it makes me drive harder than ever. I knew Jon believed in me, I knew Steve did too, but I didn't know how much he believed in me and the look in my team's eyes when we did this video let me know I couldn't slow down, I couldn't stop, I couldn't give up and, most of all, we were on a mission to make an impact and change lives. The way my team believed in me was a feeling that I didn't know I would feel twice in this lifetime.

21

IF YOU WANT BLESSINGS, BECOME A BLESSING FOR OTHERS. THE MISSIONS TO SERVE

I had many things that were going in the right direction, I started to get more involved in our church, Park Valley Church, and this is exactly what I needed in my life. Park Valley Church would help change my life and save my marriage. I started to serve at Park Valley Church and get more involved. You see serving for me is easy. I know for a fact that God blesses those that put others first. Proverbs 11:25-Those that refreshes others, themselves will be refreshed. One of Park Valley's missions is to serve. The Bible says to love others as you love yourself and it is easy for us as humans to love ourselves. We just need to love others the same. Things were going well and the video for Caliber turned out great and from the comments it inspired many. This was inspiring to me as I received so much love from the videos. Through the video process I realized that there are many that were watching me directly to see how far they could go in the company and more than that some were looking at that on a life level. I also found that we all have followers and on some level we are all leaders as others look up to us. It could be at work, in your community, church, neighbors, and family. Financially things kept getting better and Tracy and I were getting closer. I still had my days when I wondered what it would be like living in Atlanta; however, I had prayed for things to turn around. I realized I couldn't focus on where I was and Atlanta too, I would have to pick a focus and work toward that goal. We were living comfortably in the townhome we were renting. Church was going great and the kids were happy, and work was going well. Why move to Atlanta at this time? I was in a mindset of if it isn't broke don't fix it.

As we went to church more and more and got deeper into God's word there was something that clicked. Park Valley was looking for volunteers to help. I sat in the audience for many Sundays thinking that I couldn't make a difference, that they didn't need my help. This went on for months and then one Sunday I decided to talk to Tracy about it. I had to open my view, it wasn't Park Valley that could use my help directly, and it was what God could use me for and how I could help others as I changed. Park Valley decided to build a bigger and newer church building attached to the old church building and so they had decided to take the church into the high school up the street from the original church building during the construction period. On Sunday mornings we would get there at 6:30 a.m. and unload trailers and take the desks out of the classrooms, move tables from the cafeteria, set up audio equipment and do our best to turn the school into a church. Park Valley was all about making this experience into a church experience, we had a lot to set up and break down every week. That sounds like a lot of work, right? It was one of the most rewarding things I have done serving in my life as I didn't think I could make a difference and have a positive impact on God's kingdom and sharing the love of Jesus. It became very hard not to attend and help on the Sundays that I was busy. If I couldn't make it, I would miss it and feel like I was missing something in my week. It is amazing how God can connect you to your purpose in life and I had found mine, it was based on serving.

I had listened to a radio show every morning from a local channel that had 15 minutes of inspiration every morning. I didn't realize the host had such a testimony. I would listen to his story and inspiration between 6:00 a.m. and 6:15 a.m. every morning and I liked what he was saying. He talked about his hard times and how he was homeless at one point. He would talk about that often and, truth be told, it was inspiring to hear that someone so successful struggled so much. I started to relate to his story around the struggle and he talked about how God changed his life. I started to think, *If God can do it for him what does He have planned for me?* It is amazing how I could only know someone as the comedian they were and not even scratch the surface of who they really were as a man. I am not one to judge people, but to not even think the process of life had taken him through the mud. Time went on and I listened to him every morning.

I found over the years that I liked to write and tell stories; however, I had no idea the impact a share from me could make. I had been typing motivational messages every day for years. My messages on social media would normally consist of a great morning to the world and thanking God for the blessings and have a topic attached, whatever I heard or whatever was on my heart. The more I typed these messages the more I found that people like them as people would tell me directly or if I skipped a day, they would say, "Eric, what happened this morning? I missed your message today." Like serving, it helped me more than it helped others. I would continue to learn that as God's word says as we refresh others we will be refreshed. I found the more I poured into others' lives, the greater mine seemed, and when I looked at my problems, I realized I didn't have major problems.

Park Valley Church started to help my outlook on life be that much better. It was as if God Himself was saying directly to me that I needed to be there. It was so automatic; Tracy and I had a tough time with this. You ask yourself how you and your wife could have a hard time with you serving in the church. Well, in life I now know that we all grow spiritually on different levels and at different times. The tough thing for any husband that takes off spiritually before his wife or any wife that takes off before her husband is that there is probably going to be some tension around it. I didn't think there could possibly be tension around God, but it is true. In life, when one feels like they are not getting the attention they would like or need, things get tense. It wasn't that I didn't invite Tracy to go to church and serve with me, it was that it felt so great to be a part of something that was so great and it served a purpose that our God designed—there was no greater feeling. I also had to understand we had children at home, and I was leaving before they would get up and this left that duty to Tracy alone, which is never fair. God helped me see this as I served. He doesn't want us struggling in our marriages, we must find balance.

With Tracy and my relationship being so rocky for so many years I felt like I couldn't depend on it and I started to learn God has to be our rock and foundation. It was crystal clear and so for this reason I would seek Him with my life and all my heart. The more I served the better I felt. We had found a church that our kids loved and Tracy and I loved. My hope was that she would start serving some day and we could serve together. I was doing my best to take care of the family and be the leader God intended me to be as I learned. It always seemed like things would go well at work or home, but at church, while serving, things always went well as God was using me to help advance His kingdom. There were days I would go into church at 6:30 and set up and stay until 1:00 p.m. and not even think about the time. I wanted to be a great example of what I should be doing, and it was fun and rewarding spiritually.

Things really were taking off with the promotion at work and how much I was grinding both in personal and professional life. I wasn't tracking progress at all, I was grinding; if something needed to be done then it got done. No matter the time or place when it came to home, work or church. It felt great that my life wasn't necessarily back on track but making progress one day at a time. The quote "inch by inch everything is a cinch" really started to set in with me day in and day out. It made sense; when climbing a mountain, focus on one step at a time and many steps will overcome or accomplish the goal of climbing the mountain. Listening to Pastor Barry in church every weekend started to change my view of God, marriage, and being a father. He truly changed the way I looked at things and my role in life and God's kingdom. Growing up there was a certain way to speak in church, there was a certain way to act, but Pastor Barry is so down to earth and approachable and real. He would preach on how he is the one with the most problems of us all. That meant something to a guy like me because growing up pastors always seemed like their life was always on top. I am not saying that in a judgmental way, but he is so real, I started to think, *Man... I can go out and start preaching the gospel in my own little way and start to make a difference in others' lives.* Pastor Barry is super sharp in the word of God, he wants people to believe, believe we can make a difference and we can become anything through God's grace and mercy that we want to become. He will also be the first to support something that God has put on our hearts to do. As the Bible says, "I can do all things through Christ, whom strengthens me." This verse goes to show that with God anything is possible. I truly believe that God created each of us with purpose and when we naturally acknowledge our gifts and start to live our purpose, it is one of the greatest joys there are. It reminds me of the saying, "We can't know where we are going until we know where we've been." I continued to serve at "PVC" and was blessed to go on a few mission trips and help some people. Not help them because it made me feel good but help them because I really believe we are all doing life together and it was the right thing to do. One great thing about serving is we never know when we will be in need. Tragedy never is expected or asked for from the ones that it hits.

One mission we went on took us to West Virginia due to flooding. This was my very first mission with PVC and let me tell you it was an experience. When they first asked me to go, I was hesitant. I really was. It is never convenient to set aside time on a weekend when you have a family, but something told me to go and it was only a down and back early morning to late night trip. Tracy's support for me serving changed. Not that she didn't ever support it, but it was almost as if God put it in her heart to understand I would be gone to help some others and she started to smile toward it. I did have to understand that every Sunday for me to be gone from early morning to afternoon could be a bit tough; she was getting the kids ready for church and they were having lunch without me. I think in every situation there are multiple views. As we took this trip I found out that truly serving is about helping others, but most of the time both people are equally blessed, the person who came to help and the person who received the help.

This is the first time I have ever seen what flooding can do to a home, property and buildings and I was in shock. One of the things that help us survive, which is water, can come into our lives and destroy everything that we have worked for and in extreme cases kill humans. Before we left I remember the PVC

Disaster Relief Team leader speaking up and saying, "Make sure you are in prayer on the way there and days before as we were going to see some things spiritually that will make us struggle," and he was right. Seeing the people who were affected by the storm and the water broke my heart. We saw people's homes that had been flooded completely from the basement to the second floor. Water had destroyed their homes, books, pictures, clothes, furniture, home foundations and other things. As I helped, I watched a wife sit in a chair as we brought items out for her to glance at them to decide if we needed to throw them out or try to save them. This was rough. They had a lifetime of memories in these boxes and things that we had to throw out for trash. There was military support in this town with bulldozers picking up trash in piles and taking it out. A few weeks before, all these items were being used or were untouched and now it was all destroyed. These times make people think, *Well, it could always be worse; I am still alive,* and that is indeed a fact. I started to understand more and more that things can be replaced and repurchased; if we have life we are blessed.

This mission's test and witness will make me and others count our blessings daily. This was my very first mission and it was mind blowing as I had never seen anything like this before. There were moments that I knew were complete God moments on this mission, one of them was when we were on our way back home and most were sleeping in the van; a few were awake and most woke up and we started talking about how we were led to PVC and started going there on a regular basis. We talked for about 15 or 20 minutes and then the van went completely quiet again and most went back to sleep. That is just like our God to discuss what brought us all together or how. It is amazing how He will use different things to get the attention of those He is going to use for the future, and He grows us and puts us right in the very spot we need to be in. This could also include speaking in front of thousands of people even when I have anxiety issues especially when public speaking; but, again, when God's got us, He's got us.

When we returned a couple of weeks later, it was time to share with the entire church what we had done as a church and explain details and the leader of (PVC DRT), Eric A, who is an awesome leader and great brother in Christ, couldn't speak at all during the services for the church and so he asked if I wanted to do it. I found a bunch of excuses as to why I couldn't do it and then something clicked. The only way I would ever get better at public speaking was to practice the very thing by doing it. It would be scary stuff to step outside of my comfort zone rather than sitting back and watching someone else do it. I also re-membered my training at Caliber. It is great how this training stays with me day to day in different situations and circumstances. It was time for me to stop worrying so much and start jumping in. I saw that God wanted me to go on this trip and speak to others for a reason and if I could accomplish this, then what else did He have waiting for me to work on within myself? I never thought my prayers were good enough to help someone have hope; I never thought that God would use me to help others see the work that He is doing in me and how He could to do the same in each and every person on Earth. It is great how we can see the very thing and work through love that God will do in others thinking it will never happen within us. I started to understand how God likes to use people that are broken and repair us, so He can get the praise and the glory. I didn't realize that the more I prayed and practiced walking with God the more I would actually start to believe on a deeper level and my faith would grow even deeper.

The second mission we went on was closer to home and I didn't realize how many people in need were right in our area and that this would lead to some greater thoughts and possibly an outreach in the future that could help thousands; I needed to remember God can do so much with so little. PVC had decided that around the holidays we would purchase pre-packaged meals that included an entire family dinner and hand-deliver them to certain addresses that we had acquired from various sources that could use some help. Here is the first great thing about this mission. I didn't want to take off work. It happened to be around the last few weeks of the year and there is never a good time to take off work, or should I say it never feels like the right time, but I found out quickly that a mission that God sets up is a great time to take off work. I didn't know this; however, we were delivering meals to old neighborhoods I used to live in, and my direct area was West Gate and Iron Gate neighborhoods in Manassas. I never knew this day would turn out like it did.

As we delivered meals, we would give toys and meals to the kids and pray with the families. The need and the giving part are God's way of building the moment to share the love of Christ and let people know that they have a place with God and He has them covered no matter what the circumstance or situation. As we drove through the neighborhoods I was touched at the need, but I also remembered the very needs that we had and that made me want to push harder and love deeper—the needs we used to have we now got to help others with. On this day, I remembered I had a cousin in this neighborhood that I was close to at one time and we always showed love and respect to each other. He was a single father and always did such great things for his kids; however, he had been having a tough time physically with arthritis over the years. We used to work together at the cable company, we would hang out and play pool and he could cut hair better than just about anyone I knew; unfortunately the arthritis had gotten a lot worse and he didn't cut hair any longer. He is such an amazing and loving father. I knew he lived in this neighborhood; however, I didn't know where. As we delivered these meals we were down to the last meal and the person who was supposed to receive it wasn't home. This left us with a meal that we needed to deliver to someone. The guy who was with me said, "Let's just find someone to give it to." He said, "I know there is someone out here that could use it, let's just ride around until we see someone," as it was middle of the morning on a weekday.

I told him, "I know my cousin lives over here, but I am unsure where and I know he is a single father and it isn't about if he needs the meal, more of helping as we all could use a little help now and then."

We found a guy outside and parked and walked up and people are normally standoffish as they do not know who we are. We said, "Sir, would you like a meal? We are from Park Valley Church helping people out here and we would love to give this to your family."

The gentlemen almost seemed offended. His exact words were, "I do not need free food; I have plenty of money."

I said, "Okay, sorry to bother you."

Then we said, "Do you know anyone who could use a meal?"

He said, "Well, I do. Do you see that yellow house over there with black shutters?"

We looked behind us and said, "Yes."

He said, "Well, that guy is a single father." He continued, "He used to be a barber and doesn't work anymore."

I said, "Don't tell me, his name is…"

He said, "Yes, it is, do you know him?"

It turns out this man out of all the places and people in this neighborhood pointed me right to my cousin's home that I felt on my heart could use this meal that I wanted to give him as God had put it on my heart. We knocked on my cousin's door and I hadn't seen him in years and we walked in and spoke with him and asked if he could use the meal and, more importantly, could we pray over him. We prayed with him and it was a reminder that God is so special, He is so amazing and with Him all things are possible. My cousin hadn't known that I was growing in my faith; last time we talked I am not even sure he knew that I pray on a regular basis. I say all this not for any glory for myself but to say others around us can feel God's love through us as we grow. It was never about the meal, never about the gift, it was about praying with my cousin. It is the change in us that others see that helps them believe! This was a local mission and it was clear to me that I could help advance the Kingdom of God by going out in the street to love those that are in need and there are so many that need. I have still had many needs on a daily basis, but I know for a fact that the only one that matters is God's love and acceptance of us. Here I went from hesitating to do this mission because of the close of the physical year and month. I must give credit to my friend, Jon Hart, whom I mentioned prior to now. When I called him and said, "I really want to do this, but the timing is off," he said to me, "Do what you feel in your heart you should." That was the end of the conversation. That is one of the many things I love and respect with Jon; he pushes you to do what you feel. He understands that we all have purpose in life and not just in work.

Another mission I was blessed to go on was to Texas. This was a bigger mission than the others; however, no more important or less important, it is just that the logistics were deeper. We as a church during the hurricane in Texas thought we would bless some people with supplies and teams to pull up beside people and pray with them as there were many people in 2017 who were affected by the storms that came through. Many lost their homes; all possessions they worked hard and some all their life for were gone within a couple of days because of the storms and flooding. We wanted to load up two 26-foot moving trucks full of supplies as a church and as a community. Well, the two quickly turned into four because of the heart of Park Valley Church and the need was so great. So, we would drive these

trucks from northern VA into Southern Texas and set up distri-
bution centers at different churches around the city of Houston.
We would also have a van that would follow the trucks for us to
swap out drivers and get rest and ensure that we all could go.
This mission had a lot of moving pieces and they called me to
ask if I wanted to go. In honesty, when I thought about driving a
truck and a 24-hour straight drive in a 26-foot truck it didn't
seem attractive at all; however these missions are never about being attractive, looking or feeling good. They are always about the
need and sharing the love of Jesus.

I remembered calling Tracy and asking her what she
thought, and her exact words were, "When are you leaving?" I
realize for me to be out at any point doing work for God she will
have to hold it together at home. I often think, *She will have the
kids all day every day while I am gone; if something needs to be
done, she will have to do it.* I do not believe everyone gives the
consideration that is needed when wanting to do something, regardless of whether it is mission work, hobbies, etc. It takes two
to take care of a family. Really more than that, but I am sure you
get the point. The fact that she completely understands what
God has placed on my heart means so much to me and in our
tough times, I remember times like this when she was there for
me in major ways and supporting me to do what God has put on
my heart.

The plan was to pull out of the church around 4:00 a.m. give or take and that is exactly what we did. This ride was going to be a long one, but some of the people who went to West Virginia were also on this mission, which was great for us to be able to serve together again. When you have served with someone prior, you start to understand the person's heart and it makes it easier to have conversations and open up to them. I believe, in most missions doing God's work, at some point there is a special moment and you know exactly why you are where you are. That is what I call "the fruit". I believe as we go through life there is "fruit" that we can and should get out of the situation or circumstance. Sometimes the fruit is for us and sometimes it is for others, but either way most of the time there is "fruit". So as we were driving down the road about an hour or so into our trip, Joe and I started to talk a bit about life. We had been on the West Virginia trip and as we started to talk and share stories about our lives we found that some of our walk in life was parallel as far as our struggles; he has a testimony from a time in his life when God absolutely confirmed that his work wasn't completed yet that would give the average person chills while listening. I know it did for me and I bet you my mouth was hanging open as he told me his story about how he was very close to death, within minutes, and the doctors saved him. Think about that for a moment; how would you view life differently if you had come close to the end within minutes? What if God has saved us many times from those minutes and never, ever even let us know we were that close?

So, as we drove, I discovered that many of the troubles that I had—relationship issues, losing the home, struggles with the family—this man had been through it and was back on his feet and then he begin to share the story of "Job" in the Bible with me. I had never read or thought deeply about "Job" at all nor did I know much of what he went through. This was the second time I'd heard of his name and how someone I respected like the story and so I thought it was time that I read Job. So, again, just like the West Virginia trip, here we are in the dark driving to do God's work and I found myself sharing my story and listening to others knowing that God wanted us to share this moment, knowing that the trip wasn't about taking the items to Texas, it was about the love for others and committing to doing God's work, but this is that "fruit" I am speaking of. This is one hour into a 24-plus-hour drive and my eyes are wide open and my ears as well, not to mention my heart.

We received so much love as we stopped in the many towns on the way to Houston on this mission. We switched out drivers and people and it was a great time to connect with many that I didn't even know who attended Park Valley Church. As we are blessed to have over three thousand members, many of us do not know each other. I learned and continue to learn that many of us struggle with the same things, a lot of the details I am sharing in this book someone has gone through or is going to go through and I really believe that. This is one reason I am writing this book, to let others know it is okay to share, it is okay. Whatever you are going through, you too will be okay; you must put God first and then life gets so much better and it is more obvious why we are here. People want to know why, what is our purpose, and God has the answer; understand that if we turn to others to ask our purpose it will be based on how they feel and that usually varies from person to person. Serving is one of the best places to start working on your heart to clear out the focus on self. There is something that happens that is so special as we bless others and put them first. Proverbs 11:25 has become one of the most impactful verses to me: Give it away as the generous shall prosper; those that refresh others themselves will be refreshed. Our hearts clear out and the blessings of the Lord come upon our hearts.

Here we are after so many tough times. Serving the Lord and going to church as we should to help keep our faith strong and to get the education we need from the Bible. We have been blessed with another home, both Tracy and I are working, and we have resources financially to allow us to share with others and provide for our family. God showed up in a major way to help us with the purchase of another home that confirmed we are exactly where we are supposed to be. We started to look into renting a bigger place as my dad was moving in with us again. I felt it was the right thing to do to invite him to live with us and as we did the right thing a good friend Kristian Smith, who is a great realtor, asked me why we would look to rent instead of buying. The monthly payment to rent was around the same price as a mortgage at the places we were looking at. I was a bit scared to commit, given our past. God will use your past to help you think and turn to Him for your next move in life. We had a little money saved up but nothing of what we would need to have a down payment on a place. This is where God showed up in a major way as He has done time and time again. At the same time of thinking of purchasing a home those same stocks someone had blessed us with years prior refinanced and we received a check that was twice the amount of our closing cost for our home, which was by far the largest check we have ever received at once. This was an amazing display of how God blesses our mission and His power is limitless.

It is so important to have the right people in your life and your heart in the right place as well. Kristian was a good enough friend to ask without prying about us purchasing a home, instead of allowing us to throw money away on rent. This was only a good idea if we had the resources, however thousands per month paid out for rent can be used in the right way for an investment.

Sometimes being educated on options and processes can make the difference in a situation. After all, we don't know what we don't know. This would also help prevent us from having to move again anytime soon.

22

Don't Stop; Keep Serving

We moved into our home that we were blessed with. At this time Tracy and I are connecting on levels that we never have before and we understand that God must be at the center. We have to build on His word, His love and His direction. I found that many years went by with struggles and as much as I prayed for God to change her, there was some changing I needed to do within my heart. I also started to pray for her heart, which I hadn't done in the past. We have now served together at a couple of outreach events through Park Valley Church, which feels amazing. Tracy has really changed and grown and we both continue to grow together. The twins are now grown men and doing really well in life, they are 24. They are active in their community and work with children. Trey is now 18 and Torie is nine years old. Things are going well at work and with my career. I am blessed that God has saved me and I know He has an amazing plan for the future. My relationship between me and my in-laws, which include Judy, is amazing as we have worked through many things over the years. I love her like a mom and do my best to look out for her whenever I can.

As you read this book I pray that something in here touches your heart and helps you believe that if you are in a struggle God will bring you through any and every situation and circumstance that life will bring you to. We are currently starting a non-profit together as husband and wife. It is called Paul's Treasures, named after Tracy's grandad. I truly believe my mission is to get into mentoring in my life. God has used my worry, my faults, my issues, my weaknesses, my anxiety, and my learning disability and has allowed me to become one of the leaders in my community, a helper in my church, a leader spiritually in my home and for my family and allowed me to write this book that hopefully will help someone do better and be better. Never let anyone tell you that you cannot be anything or will never be anything. It is up to God to bring you through whatever appears to be a roadblock. We must give Him praise and glory; we must lean on Him and not our own understanding. Our marriage is getting stronger with time because of God. When I look back at all the time that we have spent together, I think *Was it a waste of energy?* No is my answer. Whenever you have two people come together and live as one, if we do not have a common focus, God being that focus, we will struggle. While leaning on God and learning purpose we learn patience and understanding. The Bible says, "A home built on a divided foundation cannot stand." God continues to work through me and is helping me daily overcome the struggles that many generations have struggled with. I have been blessed by him to say NO MORE, no more cheating, no shortcuts, no more of my family's generations doing the very things that held us down by being selfish and not thinking of others. Because it must stop, it stops here. Sometimes we pass on the very pain that we hated and hurt deep down inside. I want a better life for my kids; I want my wife to have a better husband; I want my children to have a better father, a better home to live in spiritually and the example of what I should be, not wishing what if I could be.

"So, as a man thinks, he shall become." I was blessed to be shown a motivational video while at a training at work by David Adams. I mentioned his name because what he showed us that day in class has helped me change so much about how I think, how I view life and, most of all, what is possible. I mentioned the radio messages in the morning. One day, while in a class, David, who I had just met a day or so before as it was a five-day class, said at break, "Have you guys ever heard of a certain message online?" Many of us said no, so he went on the web and brought up a video and put it on the projector screen. And WOW this guy's passion, voice and intention are amazing, I have never heard anyone speak with such, I have never seen anyone walk with such. I started to watch these videos, which led to other motivational messages. I mention this because I love to listen to motivational messages daily and they are helping change my thought process. Yes, I said daily, so I started to understand myself a little more. I believe in life it is so important to understand what pushes you, your why, how you operate. I think a lot of times many of us do things we do not like to do, we do things that do not connect with our whys, our purpose, our vision, and that is when the richest person can be empty, the person who should have many things to celebrate can feel empty. Money is important, yes, but the most rewarding is purpose. Purpose leads to legacy and helping others help themselves. So I have listened to these messages for years and they have helped inspire me to write this book as well through their messages; I now use the very tough and timely commute in northern VA to inspire myself through these messages and to inspire others—as I learn I share. That is an example of how you can take something that seems to be a pain and inspire many through the share, but most of all, if I didn't listen, if I didn't pay attention, I would never be able to share. As I mentioned earlier about learning self, I found that I learn better, deeper from the tone and the voice of the messenger. I also learn better through listening and seeing than reading. If you are struggling with something, maybe it isn't that you aren't good at it, maybe it is time to try another source or avenue.

As you have read there are so many things that could have gone worse. Being in the wrong place at the wrong time, being associated with people I shouldn't have, all that could have gotten me in so much trouble, possibly jail, hurt, addicted to drugs or, even worse, dead by association. It is important that we make smart decisions. I was always one to believe that just because I am not doing it directly I will be okay; that is not true, so many are in trouble today by association and it is real. My message to the younger people, teenagers, young adults and all: Keep your focus and know that just because you didn't get in trouble yet doesn't mean it isn't coming by hanging with those that break the law or do things they shouldn't do that includes hurting others. It was God's grace and mercy that kept me. He will do the same for you, but it isn't necessary to go down these dead-end streets that end badly for so many.

By no means do I have it all figured out, but I glorify God in all that He has done and continues to do in my life. A few thoughts I humbly and gracefully have are who would have thought that Tracy and I would be celebrating 18 years of marriage this year and that in my toughest times of need, during the bankruptcy, an investment would have been made on my behalf because of the commitment to the Lord and He not only saw it coming, but He made it happen. There is no other explanation as the persons who made the investment had no idea that I was going through bankruptcy and one day that investment would allow me to write a personal check to pay off one of my vehicles and to write a check to cover the closing cost for our current home. Who would have known that the house we loved so much would be replaced by another house as the address isn't as important as the love in the house to make it a home? I will tell you who … GOD. He has been with us every step of the way and I can see it all so clearly now. So here we are today and these are some of the reasons I wake up every day and thank the Lord for the day and the blessings. I cannot take the credit but share how blessed I am by His grace. I have been blessed to get promoted within my company, the largest collision repair organization in history; they have included me in three motivational videos that they have produced now. I have an amazing team at work that supports me and believes in me. My team and I won an award at work after being promoted to regional manager and as top regional manager in 2017 and won a trip to Miami, FL with Tracy and we got to spend time all-expenses paid hanging out with the top leadership of the company. I currently oversee six locations, managing and overseeing all production in these locations, which includes a large amount of revenue.

I am currently studying ministry and sharing the gospel daily in many ways and on many levels. I may be being called to full time ministry one day along with being a public speaker and motivator. I have spoken a few times at PVC; that means despite the anxiety of public speaking I have spoken in front of 3,000 plus and actually enjoy it now. I have taken my daily written messages that I spoke of on social media and I share videos daily on the social media platform, which has helped me in many ways and helped others too judging by the comments that I receive on a daily basis.

God has shown me exactly what I should be doing and where I should be doing it in this season; He has helped me to overcome my learning disability and all of the doubt and worry of not being good enough to grow and go some of the places I have been in and understand that life is about people, not a test or a piece of paper. My marriage has been blessed so much with understanding and love over the years; I have been blessed with amazing kids who are healthy and who I love very much. I can provide for them not just in a monetary way but with the love and the guidance that any parent would want a child to have as that is what many of us wanted growing up. My anxiety is under control without medicating, which is amazing, I have found that anxiety has a lot to do with my breathing. Once my mind gets into a flight-or-fight mode, it wants to freeze up and my breathing gets heavy, which takes away the ability to speak properly as my brain wants air knowing I am supposed to breathe but it cannot. Once I realized this, it allowed me to slow down my talking and breathing, which helps keep my mind clear.

I must give God the praise and glory for it all. I feel complete and at peace. I feel as though God is going to continue doing amazing things in my life and the lives of those that I love very much. "Worry about nothing, but instead pray about everything." I have to tell you if you are struggling with anything, pray and put in the work for God to bless as faith without works is dead, which means I can pray about it but it isn't going to come unless I put some work into my prayer. I cannot pray for something to come to me and sit on my couch and wait. He will take limits off limitations, He will help you get to new levels, it doesn't matter your past, your color, your height, your weight, your size, your look or where you come from. Understand it takes courage to get out of your comfort zone, just to find out that zone was never that comfortable anyway. It is amazing how we can stay there until we know we must do different. God has a plan for my life just as He does for yours. We must trust Him in order to seek out those plans. I hope you have enjoyed reading this and truly find value that will impact your life in a positive way for change. Remember: as we think so are we. If we do not change the way we think, we will continue the same actions, which will recycle our experiences.

SPECIAL THANK YOU

T hank you to anyone who has touched my life in any way, which could have appeared good or bad at the time. You have helped me become the man I am today. Tracy, I love you with all my heart and I am grateful for the love and support that we share and the growth that we have both achieved over the years. You are truly my life partner and I am blessed to call you such. I wasn't always the man I should have been, but we made it through some very tough times and didn't give up on one another even when we struggled to see tomorrow. I am forever grateful. Thank you for being the mother of our beautiful children and holding it together even during the younger years when I struggled to be who I was supposed to be.

To all four of my children, I love each of you with all my heart. Justice and Justin, I apologize for not being the man I should've been earlier in your lives; however, there was a point when, through a conversation with my uncle Tony, I realized God placed you exactly where you needed to be and kept you. I am so proud of the men you have become. Continue to serve your community and those in your lives keeping God at the center of your lives. For that I am forever grateful. Trey, you are the very first one to carry my name and your grandad's first grand-child by blood and name. I am so proud of the young man you are and the huge heart of giving you have. Be sure to remember that, and that I love you very much and (ASNF- a son never forgets) it's going to be time for you to take the "Folks" torch and be all you can be, Son. Take it to another level of generations just as I have. It is not about more; it is about quality of life. Torie, you are an amazing daughter and I am blessed that you changed my life and my heart. A son is very special for sure. A daughter changes everything and thank you for doing that for me. You are a beautiful young girl, and don't you ever forget the times we spend together and how special that feels to you. I pray as you prepare to be the lady God wants you to be that He covers your choices, your decisions, your life. You are a true reflection of your beautiful mother and I am honored always and forever to be your dad. As I write this, I share tears of joy and wish we could rewind the hands of time. Children, I know each of you have a very special place in this world as you are each unique and special in your own personality. Never let anyone tell you that you cannot do something. Put God first and you will never be last.

To my parents who have always believed in me. I love you both. Thank you for all you have done and loving me to the best of your abilities. I wouldn't have had my life any other way. I am proud of you both for doing your best, loving deeper than you were loved, providing more than you have ever had. Momma, you have been the biggest example of love and grace that I have seen in my life. It is so great to see you happy and loving life. I know you have plans to retire this year. I am so proud of you and thank you for loving me in all circumstances. Dad, thank you for being my best friend that I can talk with at any time about anything. Thank you for always believing in me and showing me the example of hard work and giving it all you got and learning as much as you can. Keep pushing forward. The happiest I have seen you is when you decided to study to become a deacon in the church. Do not give up on that, there is something special there for you. You have been open and transparent with me about your life and that has helped me more than you know. I am proud of you for having the courage to change and become a better man.

To my brothers and sisters, all of you, I love you very much and hope and pray that sometimes we will all come together and have a day out together as one. Thank you for putting up with me throughout the years. We have laughed, loved and cried together. You all are the very best and I am blessed to have each of you to call brother or sister.

To my mother-in-law, Judy, I love you very much. I want to thank you for taking care of the twins and loving them as you did. I thank you for loving me as a son. Whenever times get tough, I always remember that you are counting on me to lead this family as I should. I really enjoy our time together and cherish it. All of your grandkids love you sincerely and I am grateful for the love you all share.

To my grandparents who I have been so blessed to have and spent some time with; each of you, including Tracy's grandparents, I love you very much and thank you for investing your time, love and wisdom in me.

To Grandma Henrietta, who passed away in 2011, thank you for introducing me at a young age to the Lord. You may be the one responsible for my passion and relationship with the Lord today. I learned so much from you growing up; watching you grind so hard and take care of and raise a village is one of the reasons I work so hard today. You are one of my "why's". When I feel like giving up or have a hard time counting my blessings, I think of you and how you never gave up on anything that I have seen you do. You were the rock of our family and life hasn't been the same for the family since you went home to be with the Lord. I love you with all my heart. I was born a boy and you helped me become a man.

To Pop, who passed away in 2002, I know I talked about so many different views, I still wonder to this day what kind of thoughts, past and views you had on life while here on Earth. I really wish you were here to ask you some of those questions now. I will see you in heaven someday.

To Paul, who passed away in 2003, Tracy's grandad, she loves you very much and still to this day talks about you and the love you have for her. It is amazing that you touched her spirit so deeply and provided for her. I hope to make you proud and I remember the promise I made you as if it were yesterday as you were going through your health issues. I plan to hold that promise as long as I have breath in my body and am blessed by the Lord to provide for our family. Thank you for setting the standard of who I should be and not who I was. I will do my very best to be the man I should be in Christ to provide for and support the family you spent so many years loving, caring, providing for and being the example of how many of us should be and could be as we follow Christ.

To Mary, who passed away in 2007, Tracy's grandmother, you have helped her in so many ways from my view. She loves you so much and shares that you all used to speak daily about the struggles, joy and love that you shared. Thank you for being who you are in her life and showing me grace and love. I am better because of it.

To Papa, who passed away in 2010, my mom's dad, I recently found out that you were a praying man, now I understand where I get it from. Thank you for being so graceful and for the understanding you displayed to many with love and grace.

To Grandma Shirley, it is such a blessing to sit and talk with you and to look back on the years that we spent growing together. I am so proud of you for being transparent and open. We need more people to pour wisdom into us to help keep us on the right path. You have impacted my heart and I will always remember our talks that we have, even the recent ones as they seem to get deeper. Please know that when I see you reading your Bible on a regular basis it encourages me and not just me but many. I love you very much.

To Uncle Tony, our relationship means so much to me. Our ability to conversate and focus on God's love, mercy and grace and share it with transparency and no judgment is amazing. I am so thankful that I can pick up the phone and call you and speak about anything and now I am starting to see my role in the next generation to carry the torch. It is amazing and know that your walk with God is inspiring many daily. I have seen you transform and become a man of God. Keep it up, Uncle. Much love and respect always.

To all my aunts and uncles, cousins, friends, family members, teachers, bosses past and present, and neighbors, please know that I have been touched someway, somehow by each of you and I am forever grateful for doing life at some point with each of you.

Thank you to Pastor Barry, Pastor Mark, the Park Valley Church staff, the First Impressions team, and the DRT team for helping me understand the importance and gift of serving, receiving the love of Christ and showing me grace that only God can provide. I love you all.

A special thank you to all of those who have helped me elevate my view, helping me along the way. John and Kelli Krauss, Jerrod and Jennifer Dalton, Jon Hart, Paul Krauss, Steve Welch, Christy Gaston, and my Craftsman Auto Body and Caliber Collision family. John Procacina, Paul Jackson and Kristian Smith, thank you for showing me love right where I am, your encouragement and share of faith has helped me in more ways than you will ever know. You all have helped me elevate my view of life, my vision for what is possible, the "how to" connecting what is possible. God has truly used each of you in my life to help me along the way and I am forever grateful and thankful for each of you and your families for who you are today.

Much love to all and remember together we can make a difference. There is power in meeting people where they are without judgment. As you all have read, I have shared some very deep and personal experiences in life and with God's grace working through each of you. Some days I have felt like that little boy from the hood; "When I was a child, I spoke as a child and now that I am a man, I must leave childish things alone" is a verse from the Bible that comes to my heart. I think of the days looking back, what if those people who helped me didn't help me? What if no one reached me in my time of need? Obviously I needed grace and wisdom not to repeat my experiences. There are so many that came from the same background that went to jail, or started taking drugs or, worse, are even dead because of the decisions that were made. I say all that to share the importance of reaching those around you where they are today with no judgement, with grace. As Jesus walked the earth, people assembled where he was, he didn't wait for them to come to him. It is so important that we all understand the affect we can have to completely change one's life, that is what each of you did for me and I am forever grateful. Remember the importance that each one reach one and teach one. One Vision, One goal, One God! Together we can rise above anything. It sure is a great day for a great day!

About the Author

Eric Folks was born and raised in the Northern Virginia area. He was introduced to God's word at a very young age by his grandmother. He always had dreams and goals bigger than his current circumstances and situations. He has a heart for helping others overcome and has a vision of us all helping each other to get better each day. He lived his early life struggling to learn, not realizing he had a learning disability. Although he had that learning disability, he understood God had a plan for his life. It was through his tough times and commitment to push through it all and seek God's plan after going through bankruptcy and close to divorce many times that his heart to serve would be his path to his blessings from God.

Made in the USA
Monee, IL
24 January 2020